Adrian Mitchell
the siege

A PLAY WITH SONGS

Music by Andrew Dickson

A play initiated by
The National Playwright Commissioning Group

OBERON BOOKS
LONDON

First published in 1996 by Oberon Books Ltd

521 Caledonian Road, London N7 9RH

tel: 020 7607 3637, fax: 020 7607 3629

e-mail: info@oberonbooks.com

www.oberonbooks.com

Reprinted in 2006

ISBN 1 870259 67 X

Cover design: Andrzej Klimowski

Printed in Great Britain by Antony Rowe Ltd, Chippenham.

This play is dedicated, by all who created it, to all refugees from war, oppression, torture, famine and poverty, in the hope that the luckier and wealthier countries of the world may welcome them, comfort them and give them safe homes.

the siege was commissioned by the National Playwright Commissioning Group especially for performance by schools. The initial project involved over 30 schools across the UK, 15 of which staged full-scale performances with casts of up to 300 pupils aged 11 to 19, including musicians. Many more schools will follow with productions of their own. Adrian Mitchell has created a vibrant and topical text with songs which speaks with the voices of young people. At a time when many schools are working in isolation, the project offers opportunities for collaboration between schools and professional theatres, large or small, in joint large-scale productions. For the first time, expertise and talent in a group of schools has been shared with spectacular results under the creative guidance of a leading playwright and the internationally famous composer, Andrew Dickson.

Preface

SUMMARY OF THE PLAY

The Swados family live in the peaceful town of Arden. War breaks out and the town is under siege by the forces of the province of Dower. The family endure the routine hardships of a siege and the father of the family is shot dead by a sniper. Betsy and Arlo, the Swados twins, are soon to be 16, which is military age in Arden. Their friends decide to hold a great birthday party for them, despite the shortages of everything.

Meanwhile the government of the town is toppling and is soon taken over, courts and all, by a plausible racist gangster called Dr Jameson and his sidekick, the Revd Mouth. The strongest opposition comes from Arden's peace movement, led by Dr Ingrid Simmons from the local hospital, a friend of the Swados family. As plans for the birthday party develop we discover that, on the eve of their birthday, the twins are planning to escape across the river and away from Arden to a neutral country.

Friends of the twins have decided to build a wild garden on a bomb site made of scrap sculptures of flowers, trees, animals etc. But the twins are leaving.

Jameson meanwhile is negotiating for more arms at an Arms Trade Fair in a neutral country. The party for the twins is ready to start – but then the news comes that the twins have left town. Crossing the river, they are caught in crossfire and Arlo is killed.

In a courtroom scene, Jameson as the judge is manipulating the crowd to create mob rule. But when he puts Ingrid on trial for reporting his atrocities, Betsy and the people rebel and leave for Arlo's funeral. To the funeral everybody brings amazing pieces, brightly painted, representing flowers, trees, birds, beasts etc to form what becomes known as the Jungle of Arden. The funeral turns into a party and a celebration of peace.

Scenes and Songs

ACT ONE

SCENE ONE: AN ORCHARD IN THE HILLS
Another Peaceful Day –The Swados family

SCENE TWO: TO LIBERATE ARDEN

SCENE THREE: MORNING UNDER SIEGE
Jolly Old Arlo – Betsy
The People in Heaven – Queue People and Viewers

SCENE FOUR: AN IMAGINARY FEAST

SCENE FIVE: TO THE DEATH
We'll Be Going – Jameson, Mouth, Thugs and All

SCENE SIX: THE OPEN SCHOOL

SCENE SEVEN: BIRTHDAY PLANS
It's The Loving That Matters – Gaby and Swados Family

SCENE EIGHT: MOONCRATER MARKET
Mooncrater Market – Stallholders
Think – Ingrid and Supporters

SCENE NINE: THE STARGATE CLUB
A New Face In A New Place – The Stargate Band

ACT TWO

SCENE ONE: LEAVING NOW
23rd Psalm – Mouth, Feathers and Congregation

SCENE TWO: THE POWTEX ARMS FAIR
Men In White Shirts – All

SCENE THREE: THE MINEFIELD

SCENE FOUR: PARTY TIME ONE
You Got Twins – Lucy and James

SCENE FIVE: SNIPERS ON THE HILLS
One Hundred Miles Away – Snipers
Put Me In a Boy Band – Snipers

SCENE SIX: PARTY TIME TWO
The Streets of Hell – Mike with Friends and Family

SCENE SEVEN: CROSSING THE RIVER

SCENE EIGHT: THE HALLS OF JUSTICE
Justice – Protesters
Takes A Long Time – Ingrid and Chorus

SCENE NINE: THE JUNGLE OF ARDEN
Cardboard Rowing Boat – Betsy, Arlo and All
The Jungle of Arden – Company

Characters

SALLY Swados, hospital nurse and mother in Arden
EDUARDO Swados, office clerk, married to Sally
Their children:
MIKE, a conscripted soldier, 17 to 19
ARLO and BETSY, twins, 14½ to 16
LUCY, 12 to 14, keen on dancing
KARL, 11 to 13, a moody pre-teenager
ELLI, 9 to 11, a worrier

LOUDSPEAKER (*offstage voice*)

GENERAL, in the Dower Army
COLONEL, in the Dower Army
Professor EVELYN Farnon, Doweranian historian
MARIANNA, Doweranian Public Relations Person
NEWSPAPER and TV REPORTERS ONE, TWO, THREE
DOWERANIAN GIRL

Radio REPORTER
SOLDIERS ONE, TWO, THREE, FOUR, FIVE
(Doweranian)

THREE ARDENIAN SOLDIERS
OLD MAN

GABY, Betsy's best friend, 15
JAMES, her younger brother, 13
MELANIE, her younger sister, 10

PEOPLE IN QUEUE
WAITING WOMAN
MRS CHANNER, keeper of breadshop
Her two ASSISTANTS

MAN and SECOND MAN IN QUEUE
WOMAN IN QUEUE
TV VIEWERS
THREE VOICES
FIRST CONTROLLER
SECOND CONTROLLER
SAD MAN

FIRST SNIPER
SECOND SNIPER

RADIO (*offstage voice*)

MAYOR of Arden, Carlos Leman

Dr JAMESON, political leader – can be male or female

The Reverend MOUTH, head of the
Church of Purity and sidekick of Jameson

THUG ONE, THUG TWO

REPORTER ONE, REPORTER TWO

SECRETARY

Dr INGRID Simmons, medical doctor in Arden Hospital

TEACHER

PUPILS

VISITOR ONE, VISITOR TWO, from the United Nations

ESTHER, a teenage schoolgirl

ANDREA, a schoolgirl, about 12

Market STALLHOLDERS, including:

KNIFESELLER, MILKSELLER, MYSTICAL
MARIGOLD, MUSTARDSELLER, CUSTARDSELLER,
PASSPORTSELLER, TICKETSELLER,
VEGETABLESELLER, MAGAZINESELLER,
MEDICINESELLER, WEAPONSELLER,
DRUGPUSHERS

STARGATE CLUB BAND

CONGREGATION

FEATHERS, mistress to the Reverend Mouth

Arms DEALER

Dealer's SECRETARY

MEN in suits

BARWAITERS

SECURITY GUARDS

SERGEANT

SNIPERS ONE, TWO, THREE and FOUR

POLICEWOMAN

PROTESTERS

FOREMAN and JURY

Public CROWD

Edward SANDOW, a fast-talking thief

HOUSEWOMAN

JESSIE Nola, a drug pusher

NOTE

Many performers will be able to play at three or more parts in this play. Much better to have trebling and quadrupling in casting than people who are unemployed for most of the piece.

One particular point to notice: regard casting as flexible. For instance Dr Jameson, the leader who emerges in Arden and is revealed as a corrupt gangster, can be played as male or female. Thugs and Snipers can be played by women.

Singing. Some of your best actors may not be able to sing very well. Sometimes (not always) the song can be taken by another actor. Certainly Mike, Sally, Betsy, Arlo must be able to sing their own songs.

ACT ONE

SCENE ONE

AN ORCHARD IN THE HILLS

Music — peaceful, cheerful. Lights up on the Upper Stage.

An orchard in springtime, with the Swados family sitting at a wooden table finishing a good meal. The orchard trees, with their pink and white blossoms, may be branches carried by actors. Several times in the play actors are asked to play parts of a fence, of a forest etc. This is a great help in changing scenes swiftly and in other ways which will become apparent in rehearsal. Pronounce the family Swaydoss, please.

The Swados family who are eating together are: SALLY, the mother, a nurse in the hospital in the city of Arden; EDUARDO, her husband, who is an office clerk; ARLO and BETSY, twins, who are 14½; MIKE, their 17-year-old brother; LUCY, nearly 13, who is crazy about dancing; KARL, a moody 11-year-old who wants to be a writer and ELLI, aged 9, who is a great worrier.

NOTE: when casting please note that most of the play takes place a year and a half later. Take this into account for ages of Swados children.

The Swados family live in the small city of Arden in the valley below, but like to come out to their orchard in the hills on holidays and at weekends.

MIKE: Third helpings of pudding, mum?

SALLY: All gone.

> *Groans.*

> Coffee time!

ARLO: I'm doing a story about a man who loves volcanoes but I need a good book on how volcanoes work –

BETSY: Orchard picnics are great, Dad. But when do we get a holiday abroad?

ELLI: Yeah! Florida! Disney World!

EDUARDO: I'm a junior clerk. Six kids. I can't afford a Disney film, let alone Disney World.

KARL: Why don't you win the lottery like everyone else, Dad?

MIKE: Seen this second-hand Harley. Down the garage where I work. All I got to do is work weekends –

SALLY: Mike, there's a family rule – no motorbikes.

EDUARDO: Motorbikes are murder.

SALLY: You ought to see what's brought in Emergency Saturday nights. Bikers with half their heads off.

LUCY: (*Dancing around.*) Motorbikes are stupid. Everything in the world is stupid. Except ballet.

ELLI: Ballet's really bad for you. Ballet dancers all get really skinny, like human skellingtons and they're always smoking and busting their kneebones just when they've been cast as the Sleeping Beauty –

LUCY: You read too many dumbo comics, Elli. Ballet makes the world go round –

They all talk simultaneously.

ARLO: You see I understand about red-hot lava forcing itself up and flowing all over the landscape –

BETSY: Dad I didn't mean a holiday in Outer Mongolia, I meant somewhere just a little bit abroad, like France or Italy with different food –

THE SETTING AND TIME OF THE SIEGE

The time is the present.

The town is called Arden. It lies in a valley among limestone hills. There is a river running beside the town.

Arden is in a country much like England, with similar levels of unemployment and education. But the country is undergoing an unpredictable, ever-shifting war between various ethnic and religious groups, egged on by ambitious local politicians, racists and religious bigots and supplied by the international arms trade (or defence industry as it prefers to be called). The people of Arden are about as intelligent, moral, patriotic and brave as the people of England, but they are not perfect.

THE LIMITS OF THE PLAY

This is not a play which attempts to explore the extremes of loss, grief and appalling physical suffering which characterise the wars and sieges of our time. It is a story about people caught up in a nightmare.

I have chosen to give most of the time to brave, energetic and normally cheerful and peace-loving people. And the story, while it has its dark shadows and murderous villains, is a positive one which culminates in a vision of possible peace, if not peace itself.

Adrian Mitchell

ELLI: I know there's queues and queues at Disney World but I wouldn't moan if I had to queue for a day at a time, my friend Mel went and she was doublestuperated –

MIKE: You get a bike. If you're a nutter, you're dead. If you got a bit of common – you take care yourself, don't you?

KARL: You know why we don't win the Lottery? You know why? Cos we don't flaming do it, that's why!

LUCY: I'm not going to argue about ballet. It's just the most beautiful thing in the world, that's all ballet is. Shut up and listen!

EDUARDO thumps on the table. Everyone shuts up.

SALLY: The Swados family parliament! I bet they can hear us down in the city. And all the way down the valley of Arden. Let's all do something quietly together.

EDUARDO: Roll the dice. Highest decides what we do.

This is obviously a Swados family way of solving disputes. EDUARDO rolls two dice.

Five! (*Passes dice.*) Sally!

SALLY: (*Rolls dice.*) It's washing up if I win. Oh – three! (*Passes dice.*) Mike!

MIKE: (*Rolling.*) Come on, dices. Seven! Betsy!

BETSY: (*Rolling.*) I'm voting for another lunch. Boom – eight! Beat that, Arlo.

ARLO: (*Whispers to dice.*) My twin sister got eight. Beat that for me. (*Rolls.*) Eight! Lucy!

LUCY: (*Rolling.*) It's a dance if I win. Three! Karl.

KARL: (*Rolling.*) We'll all have a go on the Lottery. Hey hey – ten! Elli.

ELLI: I dunno what I'll choose. (*Rolls.*) Ooh – six six
  – twelve!

EDUARDO: Elli wins. What do we all have to do, Elli?

ELLI: (*Can't decide.*) Oh – I'll let Mum choose.

  Groans.

SALLY: We'll sing together.

  Any of the family who plays an instrument picks it up.

ANOTHER PEACEFUL DAY

FAMILY: (*Sing – individual lines to be assigned.*)
  High above the city of Arden
  The hill is misty and steep
  In the yellow sun of the morning
  It looks like a lion asleep

  All the hillside pathways are zig-zag
  It's easy losing your way
  But we will climb up to our orchard
  To witness the blossoms of May

  Sitting round a table under pink and white trees
  Eating very slowly, enjoying each bite,
  Sitting round a table with our memories,
  Terrible and happy, from morning till night.
  Sitting round a table under pink and white trees
  On a hill above the city of Arden.

  Sitting round and arguing the rights and the wrongs.
  Pass the roly-poly. Let's have some more cheese.
  Harmonising sweetly on our favourite songs.
  Drinking wine together, the pink and the white –
  Sitting round a table under pink and white trees
  On a hill above the city of Arden.

Another peaceful day *
Feels like another peaceful day
And our troubles float away
And it's another peaceful day
On a hill above the city of Arden

There is a noise of a spluttering car engine getting nearer. The sound of a loudspeaker.

SALLY: What's that?

MIKE: Looks like a loudspeaker car. Like they have at elections.

EDUARDO: There's no election. Shut up. Listen.

LOUDSPEAKER: (*From off.*) This is an emergency. Enemy forces have surrounded the city of Arden. Return to your homes immediately. Wait there for further information. This is an emergency. Enemy forces have surrounded the city of Arden. Return to your homes immediately. (*It keeps repeating.*)

EDUARDO: Quick, everyone. Get packed up.

SALLY: Don't bother with plates. Come on.

FAMILY scramble to get their stuff together.

ELLI: Is it a real war?

MIKE: Looks like it. Could be a siege.

EDUARDO: Quick.

EDUARDO and SALLY herd family down from Upper Stage, carrying rucksacks etc. As they reach lower level, LUCY suddenly turns and runs up again before anyone can stop her.

SALLY: Lucy, come back.

---

* *This chorus to be sung in counterpoint with the two Sitting Round verses.*

LUCY: I left my ballet doll.

LUCY arrives at the orchard. She gets down to retrieve her ballet dancer doll from under a bench. When she stands up she is faced with three enemy SOLDIERS with guns, emerging from the trees. The four all stare at each other. LUCY screams, turns and runs down to join her family. No shots are fired. More SOLDIERS emerge, dismantle the trees in blossom and place sandbags etc. to form a gun-emplacement and sniper post at one end of the Upper Stage. The loudspeaker announcement continues, fading into the distance. Strong, dark music.

SCENE TWO

TO LIBERATE ARDEN

Upper Stage. Lights up at the other end of the Upper Stage – where the SOLDIERS aren't. A GENERAL in fatigues, a smarter COLONEL, EVELYN Farnon (a historian) and MARIANNA (a public relations woman) sit at a table, on the front of which is the national flag of Dower, the besieging province. Behind them is a map which shows the city of Arden surrounded by forces on the hills and mountains. A river runs beside the city. TV lights on the party at the table. On the Lower Stage, just below the Upper Stage, a group of newspaper and TV REPORTERS.

MARIANNA: All right, ladies and gentlemen of the media, welcome. This is a crucial date in the history of the province of Dower. We'd like to explain why it's been necessary to place a military ring around the city of Arden. I shall ask the Doweranian historian, Professor Evelyn Farnon, to sketch in the background.

EVELYN: Thank you, Marianna. As you know, Arden was originally founded by craftsmen from the state of Dower in the middle ages. Today the city still has a minority population of Doweranians. Historically this minority was often maltreated. But in the past five years the Ardenians have increasingly persecuted our people because of their race, culture and religion. I hope you all have a copy of this Report on Atrocities in the City of Arden (*Waves a big typed book.*) – eyewitness accounts by oppressed Doweranians.

DOWERANIAN GIRL: (*Appears suddenly at the table – evidently well-rehearsed.*) They took my little sister away. They said they were taking her to hospital. I walked through the snow to the hospital. But she wasn't there. Then I saw her body in the car park on the back of a truck. Her mouth was open and she was dead.

REPORTER ONE: What was your sister's name?

Embarrassing pause.

MARIANNA: Sorry, we don't have time for questions now. Colonel?

Exit DOWERANIAN GIRL.

COLONEL: (*Something of a smoothie.*) I'm happy to report that so far Operation Nightingale – designed to protect Doweranians from further atrocities – has been carried out with surgical precision. The city of Arden is surrounded. All supply lines are cut. Now it's simply a question of time...

REPORTER TWO: So it's a siege and you'll starve them out?

GENERAL: We're not just sitting around in the hills. We've got planes at work you know, and rockets – all be over in a couple of weeks.

REPORTER THREE: There've been reports of cluster bombing –

COLONEL: Negative. We've been very very careful in air attacks to avoid collateral damage –

REPORTER THREE: You mean killing civilians?

COLONEL: Affirmative. We're doing everything we can to conduct this siege humanely.

REPORTER THREE: How many people have been killed in this first week, then?

GENERAL: Absolutely no idea. We're not going to get into that body-count business. Body count means absolutely nothing.

Lights down on the Press Conference. Lights up on SOLDIERS the other side of Upper Stage. They are sitting around casually, being interviewed by a Radio REPORTER who moves from one to another.

REPRTER: What do you feel about shelling the city down there?

SOLDIER ONE: We're here to do a job. It's just a job.

SOLDIER TWO: Not any old job. You get a buzz out of it, up here in the hills. We're going to teach those Mudheads a lesson.

REPORTER: Mudheads? You call the people of Arden – Mudheads?

SOLDIER THREE: Sure. Always have. They live down the valley, down in the mud. Mudheads.

SOLDIER TWO: Yeah. Well they call us Gnashers. Cos they say we got rotten teeth. Ha! Look!

SOLDIERS show their teeth in big grins.

Anyhow, Mudhead suits them.

SOLDIER FOUR: Look, we've got them in a trap. We can bring the sky in on those people.

REPORTER: You've got the hardware?

SOLDIER FOUR: Beautiful stuff. We got an A10 Tank Buster with rockets. And a gun can fire armour-piercing shells at four thousand two hundred a minute.

SOLDIER TWO: Yeah. It's going to be the biggest firework display you've ever seen.

REPORTER: But why are you fighting?

SOLDIER THREE: Because we're different.

SOLDIER TWO: You mean – they're different.

SOLDIER FIVE: Why don't we be just like them, then we wouldn't have to kill them?

Other SOLDIERS laugh at him.

SOLDIER ONE: No. You know. We're here to do a job. Yeah. It's just a job.

Fade on SOLDIERS. Lights up on GENERAL's Press Conference, but a year and a half later. Some change of clothes. More weariness apparent. No EVELYN.

MARIANNA: Welcome back, folks. We've got to keep this short, the General has to fly out on a mission.

REPORTER THREE: Is that a peace mission, General?

GENERAL: Yes. I'm flying out to arrange for more troops and shells and rockets.

REPORTER ONE: It's a year and a half since you honoured us with your first press conference, General. How would you summarise progress in that year?

GENERAL: Progress?

REPORTER ONE: Progress in the siege of the city of Arden.

GENERAL: Rome wasn't destroyed in one day.

COLONEL: We've maintained the siege. We've tightened the siege.

REPORTER TWO: They're surviving the siege.

COLONEL: Surviving is the word for it. Look – all the lines to Arden are cut off. They've no electricity, no gas, no fuel. Everything's rationed. And we're dead in the middle of winter. How long would you give 'em?

GENERAL: Couple of weeks.

MARIANNA: Well, perhaps...

REPORTER TWO: Excuse me, General. Two weeks? Same as your estimate a year and a half ago.

GENERAL: I tell you they'll be starved out of that little slum in two bloody weeks. What's the matter with you? Are you a Mudhead or something?

Quick fade on Upper Stage.

SCENE THREE

MORNING UNDER SIEGE

In the city of Arden. Lower Stage. Winter. The siege has been going on now for a year and a half. One corner is the Swados home – just a kitchen table and a wood stove. The rest represents streets in the city. The sound of wood being chopped offstage. EDUARDO emerges, in suit, scarf round his neck, carrying small axe and a handful of chopped wood, puts wood in stove. Bends, lights it. Alarm clock on table goes off. EDUARDO turns it off, puts down axe.

EDUARDO: OK everybody! Six o'clock and the stove's alight. Get yourself up. Bring out your slops.

EDUARDO places an old newspaper on the floor and puts two large buckets on it. The rest of the family begin to emerge.

SALLY, first, in a nurse's uniform, empties her chamberpot into a bucket. Steam.

SALLY: I wish one of those TV interviewers would come down here and ask me: What would the lifting of the siege mean to you, Mrs Swados?

EDUARDO: What would you say, Sal?

SALLY: Peace would mean a lavatory that bloody works.

Enter ELLI, now 10, carrying chamberpot which she empties into bucket.

ELLI: Oh Mum, you swore.

SALLY: (*Starting to make porridge on the stove.*) Did I?

Enter ARLO and BETSY with chamberpots, which they empty into buckets. They are now nearly 16.

BETSY: Oh not bloody porridge again.

SALLY: Don't swear. It's good porridge.

ARLO: Not that lumpy, bitter stuff?

Enter LUCY who is now 14, with chamberpot which she empties gracefully.

LUCY: Good morning, my lumpy, bitter old brother.

MIKE, 18, in army uniform and carrying a rifle, dashes in.

MIKE: Five past six? God's teeth I'll be late on parade.

SALLY: You've got to eat something.

MIKE: Give us a spoonful.

SALLY offers a spoonful of porridge, which MIKE takes, then yells.

Yaow! It's red-hot! I'm off.

ARLO: You haven't emptied your slops.

MIKE: (*Exiting.*) I did it out the window.

LUCY: You beast.

Enter KARL, now 12, empties chamberpot.

EDUARDO: Karl. You're slopping out sloppily.

KARL: Sorry, Dad. I was born sloppy.

SALLY has served out a plate of porridge for everyone. They all stand round eating. While they eat, EDUARDO gives the orders for the day from a piece of paper.

EDUARDO: Swados family orders of the day.

Groans.

Sally and Elli – bread queue till Sally has to go to the hospital. Arlo and Betsy, water collection. Lucy and Karl – take out the garbage and get rid of it but not in the river, OK? Then collect any fuel you can get your mitts on. Bits of coal like yesterday?

KARL: What about you, Dad?

EDUARDO: After I have the pleasure of emptying the slop buckets, I'll be working down at my office. Arlo's turn to eat with me in the canteen. Seeya dead on noon, Arlo.

ARLO: Alive if possible. OK Dad.

EDUARDO exits with slop pails.

ELLI: Got the bread ration book, Mum?

SALLY: (*Rummaging in her overcoat.*) Somewhere in my coat. Here it is.

Everybody has finished their porridge now, plates stacked, everybody putting on overcoats, scarves, hats etc — it's a very cold morning.

KARL: It's freezing.

ELLI: You wait till you get outdoors.

BETSY: Snot icicles.

ELLI: Yuck!

Re-enter EDUARDO with empty buckets.

SALLY: My hero! (*Kisses him.*) Get off to work.

EDUARDO: (*Putting down buckets, picking up briefcase.*) Remember kids, it's the season for snipers — so when you cross the street — run like hell.

Exit EDUARDO to work.

ARLO: If you walk, the bullet hits you. If you run, you hit the bullet.

JOLLY OLD ARLO

BETSY: (*Sings.*) Jolly old Arlo
Jolly old Arlo
I've got a twin called
Jolly old Arlo!

ARLO shakes his fist at her, but grins. She can usually cheer him up.

SALLY: Get this table out of the way. Everybody out in the street. We've got work to do!

Table and stove cleared. Lower Stage now represents streets in the city of Arden. Machine guns hammer. Echoing thud of mortars. Occasionally the scream of a shell. First we follow ARLO and BETSY. They wheel two broken-down looking bikes. But each bike is covered with big empty plastic water cans. They wheel them a couple of times round the stage, carefully, keeping their heads down and join on the end of a queue of people waiting to get water from a standpipe, which is guarded by three Ardenian SOLDIERS. Much nearer the front of the queue is 15-year-old GABY, who is BETSY's best friend, and her 13-year-old brother JAMES, who have rucksacks with big water bottles in them. Others have invented different means. Anything is easier than carrying water by hand. When you get to the head of the queue you have to run across an open space to reach the soldiers. That's when snipers open fire. You take a chance.

SOLDIER ONE: (*To OLD MAN at the head of the queue.*) You next, chum. Get over here.

OLD MAN: Is it safe? They've got snipers.

SOLDIER TWO: Course it's not safe. Take a chance, grandad.

PEOPLE IN QUEUE: Get on with it. Hurry up.

OLD MAN: Oh God!

OLD MAN makes a dash for it. Sniper fire. OLD MAN makes it. SOLDIERS fill his bottle.

GABY: (*Seeing ARLO and BETSY, shouts down the line.*) Hey, Betsy! Arlo! Some fun isn't it!

ARLO ignores her, writing in his notebook as he waits in the queue. Some others read or chat quietly to their neighbours as the queue moves on.

BETSY: Gaby! Haven't seen you for days.

GABY: We was lucky. Got a burst waterpipe in our street. All the water you wanted. Twenty-four hours a day.

BETSY: And no snipers? That's great. What happened?

JAMES: Some bastard mended it.

BETSY: Never mind. Maybe it'll rain.

GABY: Rain? Those clouds are frozen solid. Hey, Arlo! Arlo! What you writing?

ARLO: You really want to know?

GABY: Try me.

ARLO: I was writing this: (*Reads from notebook.*) 'They blew up our church. I watched from behind a tomb, saw the coloured glass shards flying through the air, landing like daggers of raindrops, the flames licking the ancient stonework, windowleads melting, turning red in the heat. The whole boiling explosion' –

[*From a piece by Sarah Mercer of Stroud.*]

WAITING WOMAN: Look we need cheering up. Why can't you write something happy?

ARLO: Because I'm going to die.

WAITING WOMAN: Well, anyone can do that.

SOLDIER THREE: Come on, next.

GABY: Yep. That's us. Come on, hero.

GABY and JAMES dash for it. Sniper fire. They make it.

JAMES: How come it takes three soldiers to guard a standpipe?

SOLDIER ONE: I watch out for the water-tap.

SOLDIER TWO: I watch out for the crowd.

SOLDIER THREE: And I nip off for a pee.

GABY and JAMES fill bottles as queue dissolves and we move to another part of the city, losing the water queue. We go to LUCY and KARL. They have a wheelbarrow and are picking off the ground anything which could serve as fuel.

KARL: There's not much left.

LUCY: You're not looking. I found eighteen bits of coal.

KARL: Keep your voice down.

A shell screams over.

LUCY: You know what I'd like?

KARL: I could have a good guess.

LUCY: A lovely big fat shiny magazine like before the siege. With a picture of Sharon Stone on the front and a free sachet of Hollywood perfume and articles about the very latest sex techniques. What d'you miss, Karl?

KARL: I miss all those films on telly about stupid people having spikes driven through their heads by deformed maniacs. Look! Two lumps! Two bloody good lumps! (*Puts coal in wheelbarrow.*)

LUCY: Great! There's a sort of dark patch in the ground over there. Let's try some digging.

KARL and LUCY take wheelbarrow and move off the stage area.

A bread queue forms and a bread counter is seen. Near the front of the queue are SALLY and ELLI together with a friend, ten-year-old MELANIE. Behind the counter is the shopkeeper MRS CHANNER and two ASSISTANTS. A hand-made sign reads BREAD SOLD HERE. *A few loaves in sight. Weighing machines. Two SOLDIERS are also on guard.*

MAN IN QUEUE: Funny. You always bring a novel. But you never get round to reading it. You want to keep track of how the queue's moving, who's barging in.

SECOND MAN IN QUEUE: You have to watch the woman giving out the bread. Is she serving quick?

Does she keep 'em waiting? If she walks away from the counter, it's agony.

WOMAN IN QUEUE: Men are no good at queuing. They're used to thinking their time's so valuable. Women get taught by their mothers and grandmothers that time isn't what matters.

MAN IN QUEUE: Men get taught to keep their daft thoughts to themselves.

MELANIE: Is it right your Karl's taken up carving model animals?

ELLI: Not all the time. He's not going round the loop if that's what you mean.

SALLY: Lots of people are getting into hobbies these days. Siege life's so boring.

ELLI: Yeah. Some people are turning religious.

MELANIE: Yeah. And some are going woozoobalooby.

SALLY: Woozoobalooby?

ELLI: That's sort of bananas but murderous with it.

MELANIE: Like those Gnasher spies slipping arsenic in the water supply.

MRS CHANNER: I'd be much happier if you'd avoid spreading rumours in my queue, Melanie.

MELANIE: Sorry, Mrs Channer.

MRS CHANNER: How's your Michael taken to the Army, Sally?

SALLY: Like a duck to water.

MELANIE: Like a lamb to the slaughter.

A shell screams over.

SALLY: (*Suddenly very angry.*) Why did they have to pick on us? This beautiful city – (*Briefly, she cries.*)

MRS CHANNER: Let's all be very calm.

ELLI: Mum'll be all right. It's just she has to work in a hospital all hours without any water or electricity and I think she sees awful things.

SALLY: (*Gives ELLI a hug.*) I'll be all right.

She has reached the counter. MRS CHANNER is serving someone else. An ASSISTANT in a white coat who doesn't know her serves SALLY.

ASSISTANT ONE: You are registered here?

SALLY hands over her family's bread ration books.

ASSISTANT TWO: (*To MELANIE.*) No, we don't accept torn-out bread coupons. You must have your ration book.

MELANIE: (*Producing ration book.*) Here. I thought –

ASSISTANT ONE: No, Mrs Swados, we can't issue bread for the day after tomorrow.

ELLI: Look mum, they're cutting our bread.

ASSISTANT ONE takes a brown or black loaf. SALLY and ELLI watch carefully as Assistant cuts half off and puts it on the scales. Assistant slices a bit off, weighs it again.

SALLY: Watch the pointer on the machine. It didn't reach the mark. Great. We get an extra bit.

ASSISTANT ONE takes a small piece of spare bread and puts it on the scale.

ELLI: What a measly old crumb.(*To MELANIE.*) We've got a rule in our family. When you're breadshopping you can eat the little makeweight bit. But you mustn't take any off the main loaf, otherwise you might eat it all up before you get it home.

SALLY takes her bread. It's not much, but suddenly she's more relaxed.

SALLY: Thanks, Mrs Channer. Elli, you nip back home with the bread – I'll be just in time on the ward if I sprint.

ELLI: Mum. All those people in rich countries, who got heating and water and all the food they can eat – do you reckon they ever think about us?

SALLY: Course they do, Elli. They watch the news. Course they think about us.

THE PEOPLE IN HEAVEN

QUEUE PEOPLE: (*Sing.*)
I'm sure that the people in Heaven
Think about the people in Hell.
I'm sure they remember them in their prayers
And I'm sure that they wish them well.
And when the flames are burning through to your bones
And you're smothered in that sulphurous smell
It's good to be aware
That the angels up there
Think of us poor devils in Hell.

QUEUE PEOPLE and BREADSHOP PEOPLE freeze, lights half down on them. Lights up on part of Upper Stage representing a peacetime sitting room with a well-dressed, well-fed family of VIEWERS. TV is on with coverage of a siege, sound of gunfire etc, But VIEWERS are concerned with giving their shopping orders.

VIEWERS: (*Sing.*) Going down the shops
Before Top of the Pops –
Any orders at all?

Choc-rolls!
Bog-rolls!
Instant coffee!
Bring a Twix back!
And a six-pack
While you're in the offie!
Disprins and Snickers,
Disposable knickers,
Poppadoms and a vegetable curry.
A quarter of lard
And a lottery card –
Sorry – too much of a hurry.
I was nipping down the shops
Before Top of the Pops,
But I think I'll stay home after all.

Lights up on bread queue. QUEUE PEOPLE sing their verse again in counterpoint to the VIEWERS singing their verse again. Big chord. The sound of an air raid siren. Lights out on VIEWERS. QUEUE PEOPLE scramble out.

GABY steps forward and talks to the audience directly.

GABY: I dunno if you've ever been in an air raid. Just in case you get caught in one, I'll tell you what to do. First, stick yourself down a shelter. Best thing is to be in a cellar near home with friends and some family. Winter you go for months on end without ever taking off all your clothes. You never see your own body. You know it's turning into something skinny and horrible. You want to forget about it. But it itches and it aches, just to remind you it's there. And of course, it smells. But you get used to your own smell and the smell of your friends and family. Smell a stranger a mile off. (*Sniffs, laughs.*) There's a lot of boredom in air raids. You read a book, if you can get near enough the lamp. Maybe you play cards for a tin of sardines. And there's always somebody saying the same old stupid things:

VOICE ONE: (*After sound of a bomb.*) Well, somebody's caught it.

VOICE TWO: (*After sound of a shell.*) If you can hear a shell, it's not going to land on you.

VOICE THREE: You're more likely to die of hunger than bombs.

All Clear sounds.

GABY: Then the All Clear sounds. And there's always the same old argument: Do you pack up the blankets and the kids and go upstairs? Or stop in the cellar and wait for the next raid? Look, sometimes it's real fun down the shelter. Yeah. And we all sing old Beatles songs and stuff. Right? But sometimes there's a kid missing and there's screaming outside and it feels like you're stuck down in hell and you know that hell is a cold dark place where little children die.

GABY turns and walks away. Lights up on EDUARDO and ARLO edging down the side of the Lower Stage.

EDUARDO: This is it. The office canteen.

ARLO: Looks posh. What's the grub like?

EDUARDO: The porridge is more like porridge than most places. Better run this last bit.

They sprint over road and join yet another queue. Each of them produces a spoon. EDUARDO spots a friend coming out.

What's on today, Bill?

BILL: Green soup. Yellow porridge.

EDUARDO: Great.

FIRST CONTROLLER: Passes?

EDUARDO: (*Producing his.*) My pass. And a guest pass.

FIRST CONTROLLER: Who is he?

EDUARDO: (*Proudly.*) My son.

SECOND CONTROLLER: Ration card.

SAD MAN: I lost my ration card.

SECOND CONTROLLER: (*Loudly.*) What are you doing here, then? No card, no food.

SAD MAN: (*Producing crumpled paper.*) I've got a note. From the doctor.

SECOND CONTROLLER: (*Loudly.*) Get yourself down the Food Office. You'll find a queue there for Lost Ration Books.

SAD MAN: But I've got a note.

SECOND CONTROLLER: Next. Ration cards.

EDUARDO: (*Handing out his cards.*) Two portions of each, please.

SECOND CONTROLLER: (*Stamping cards.*) This doesn't entitle you to second helpings, you know.

EDUARDO: Right. (*Takes cards.*)

THIRD CONTROLLER gives them each a small bowl of soup and another of porridge.

ARLO: Green and yellow! Looks great.

EDUARDO: Come on Arlo. Get in a queue for a table.

ARLO: What's that funny queue for?

EDUARDO: That's for the canteen lavatories.

ARLO: (*Impressed.*) Proper lavatories? With water?

EDUARDO: No, they're horrible. But people, you know, people just can't wait.

ARLO: I can see that.

EDUARDO: Come on, quick, hop on the ledge.

EDUARDO and ARLO find a place to sit together, probably just under the Upper Stage.

Lucky!

They begin to eat their soup, slowly.

First time we've been alone in months.

ARLO: That's right, Dad.

EDUARDO: So tell me everything. You've had no more hallucinations?

ARLO: Those voices. No. That was when I messed with drugs. I'm OK now.

EDUARDO: So – what you going to do with your life?

ARLO: I'll be sixteen in a few weeks. They'll put me in the army.

EDUARDO: Is that what you want?

ARLO: Nope. I don't want to kill anyone. I want to write.

EDUARDO: Why?

ARLO laughs.

Am I being stupid?

ARLO: No. I want to write to stop myself going mad. Because writing is what I can do. The only way I can talk to people.

EDUARDO: Maybe it's the way you can sing to people.

ARLO: You understand a lot – for a parent.

They put their soup aside, take up porridge.

EDUARDO: That was good soup.

ARLO: That's history. Now we're doing yellow porridge.

EDUARDO: We never have time to talk about what matters.

ARLO: One day, maybe.

EDUARDO: One day, Arlo. Maybe on the day you publish your first novel. And it's called Yellow Porridge. And you take me out to celebrate at the Café Royal. With your mother. And we're taking our time over coffee and brandy and talking, with very sad eyes, about the troubles of the world. And suddenly you stand up. And you climb on your chair. And you step on to the middle of the table. And you say:

ARLO: The troubles of the world? I've just worked out how to solve them.

EDUARDO: And so me and you and your mother dance out of the Café Royal and put the world right. But first —

ARLO: But first what?

EDUARDO: First — you have to pay the bill!

EDUARDO and ARLO have finished their porridge. They throw their tin plates on the floor to the disgust of CONTROLLERS, and embrace each other.

(*Announces it to the world as they leave.*) This is my son Arlo!

EDUARDO and ARLO pause on the edge of the street.

(*Pointing.*) We're in luck. An apple seller.

EDUARDO and ARLO freeze. Keep light on them. But lights up also on TWO SNIPERS in the hills on Upper Stage.

FIRST SNIPER: Bet you can't waste a Mudhead in the next five minutes.

SECOND SNIPER: You're on. (*Aims down at street.*)

An OLD WOMAN crosses the street with a battered supermarket trolley full of water bottles.

FIRST SNIPER: How about her?

SECOND SNIPER: Nar. Could be my grannie.

EDUARDO: If she can do it, I can do it.

ARLO: It's not worth risking, Dad.

EDUARDO: Oh, your mother loves apples.

ARLO: No.

EDUARDO: Let's be brave. (*Starts to cross the street.*)

SECOND SNIPER: Here we go!

SECOND SNIPER fires. EDUARDO, crossing the street, falls, shot in the chest. ARLO runs to him, drags him over the street.

EDUARDO: Take your mother. To the Café Royal. Arlo.

Dies. A cold white light freeze to indicate the death of EDUARDO. Darkness. Clear stage.

SCENE FOUR

AN IMAGINARY FEAST

Evening. The Swados home. BETSY and LUCY Swados are sitting around with their friends, JAMES, MELANIE and GABY. Small battery radio on. End of music.

RADIO: This is Radio Free Arden with the latest news.

GABY: Oh no – save the batteries for music!

RADIO: Enemy forces concentrate heavy fire on the Cathedral area. Bread ration to be cut by half. Foreign journalists in visa row.

BETSY: Let's just get the bit about the Cathedral.

GABY: It's all the same.

RADIO: Seven shoppers were killed and sixteen injured by shells deliberately aimed at the area around the Cathedral.

GABY: And I was going down there to get my hair done.

BETSY switches off radio.

JAMES: There's more important things in the world than your hair.

GABY: Name one.

LUCY and KARL come in breathless, pushing wheelbarrow full of wood and coal.

BETSY: What've you got? That's great.

LUCY: We found this bombed out coal cellar –

KARL: – With no armed guard.

BETSY: Not bad!

ELLI: How's your mum these days, Mel?

MELANIE: Bit like a zombie. She seems to plod around the house, says nothing.

BETSY: Well, she's pregnant, isn't she?

JAMES: Seems to me the whole human race of women is pregnant!

LUCY's looking at a colour magazine, very tattered.

LUCY: Hey! Look at that!

KARL: What is it? Swan bleeding Lake?

LUCY: Much better than that. It's chicken with sausages and chips and green peas and bread sauce.

Others crowd round. It's been pertinently asked, how do you distinguish between this and the orchard picnic without using real food in the orchard. My answer would be to use imaginary food in both scenes but have the Imaginary Feast acted in an exaggerated way.

JAMES: Hmm. Not bad. Bags I the sausages.

GABY: If we're going to have a feast, let's be civilised. (*She raises an imaginary glass.*) Orange juice.

Others raise imaginary glasses.

ALL: Orange juice!

BETSY: (*Sipping.*) It's very cold. And little flaky bits of orange in it.

KARL: (*Spitting.*) I got a pip.

ELLI: Made with real oranges...

LUCY: Have another glass – (*Pours from imaginary jug.*)

GABY jumps up and goes into energetic mime.

BETSY: What's that meant to be, Gaby?

GABY: Making some more juice. Six oranges. Cut 'em in half. Switch on the juicer. Whirr Whirr Whizz Whizz.

Others join in sound effects.

Switch off. Off! Pour the juice – look at that fizzy orange foam.

JAMES: I'll make some.

ELLI: Sorry, ran out of oranges. Nip down the shop.

JAMES: That'll take hours.

BETSY: No it won't, there's no queues any more.

ELLI: Not even for oranges?

BETSY: No.

KARL: Not even for ice cream?

GABY: Nope. What flavours do you all want?

ALL: (*Shout out flavours.*) Strawberry. Vanilla. Chocolate Chip. Fudge Ripple. Tutti Frutti.

> *SALLY enters wearily in nurse's uniform, sits down, brightens up when she recognises the game they're playing.*

SALLY: I'll have a tub and a double cone and a chocbar and a lolly.

JAMES: What flavours?

SALLY: Gin and tonic.

ELLI: Can we have some croissants?

LUCY: Sure, croissants with chocolate in them.

ELLI: There's no such thing with chocolate in, you made that up Lucy.

SALLY: They have 'em in France. *Pain au chocolat.*

JAMES: Wow! Let's have some pizza!

KARL: Fish and chips!

BETSY: Onion bhaji and poppadoms and chicken tandoori and lady's-fingers and dahl and stuffed paratha and mango chutney –

GABY: And a barrel of lager –

LUCY: What? After all that ice cream?

JAMES: We'd all be sick as Michael Jackson.

ALL pretend to be sick and are falling about laughing.
Suddenly ARLO walks in silently with a bag in his hands.
ALL fall silent.

ARLO: I got us some apples.

Opens bag of apples on the table. Nobody moves. ARLO, who
is in a state of shock, silently hands an apple to each one of
them, ending with SALLY.

I've got to tell you. Dad's been killed.

ALL freeze. White light.

SCENE FIVE

TO THE DEATH

Upper Stage. Another press conference. This time the table bears the
flag of Arden. Behind the table the MAYOR, Carlos Leman, who
is honest but weak. Also, silent at first, Dr JAMESON – played as
male or female – a very formidable personality, part gangster, part
racist political leader, part academic, who has a strong following
in the town. This includes the Reverend MOUTH, the fast-talking
founder of the Church of Purity and a number of THUGS. MOUTH
and THUGS are not on the platform, but in a crowd which includes
REPORTERS. Also in the crowd is Dr INGRID Simmons, from the
local hospital, who is a member of the peace movement in Arden and
a friend of Sally and the Swados family – who aren't present.

REPORTER ONE: But how's this siege going to end, Mr
   Leman?

MAYOR: Well I'm not a clairvoyant –

REPORTER ONE: No, but you're the Mayor of Arden.

REPORTER TWO: Is it stalemate?

REPORTER ONE: Or is there any progress at all?

MAYOR: Talks are continuing.

REPORTER TWO: Talks with who?

MAYOR: International talks.

THUG ONE: (*From crowd.*) And talks with the Gnashers? Eh?

JAMESON: Now, let's have some order.

SECRETARY: Thank you, Dr Jameson. Yes, this is a Press Conference. If the public would please refrain –

THUG ONE: Are you talking to the Gnashers?

REPORTER TWO: Are you in negotiations with the Doweranians?

MAYOR: We are hoping –

MOUTH: How can our elected representatives hope to command our respect while they sit down and talk with murderers?

SECRETARY: Who do you speak for, sir?

MOUTH: I speak in the name of the Church of Purity and in the name of all right-minded citizens of Arden when I say that the Doweranian government is a criminal organisation with the blood of our women and children dripping from its hands.

MAYOR: I don't think that's a helpful contribution to our efforts –

JAMESON: This is war. Our citizens cry out for strong moral leadership –

MAYOR: I'm working for a solution. I'm not going to stand up and make blood-curdling speeches about enemy atrocities and national pride.

JAMESON: (*Quietly.*) Perhaps we need a little inspiration.

'YES' from some of crowd, including THUGS and MOUTH.

Perhaps we shouldn't be ashamed to display a little national pride.

'YES!'

INGRID gets up on the platform. She wears a white dove on her coat.

INGRID: May I say something, Mr Mayor?

MAYOR: Please. In case anyone doesn't know her – this is Dr Ingrid Simmons, who works at the hospital.

Applause.

MOUTH: And also for the so-called Peace People.

Some applause, some boos.

INGRID: Remember the times before the siege? There was a long build-up of hatred between the people of Dower and Arden. I campaigned against that. My mother was from Arden. My father was born in Dower.

Boos.

Arden, my home, has always had a wonderful mixture of races and religions. That's one of the things make it such an exciting place to live in. (*Some boos, some applause.*) I hate war and I worked to keep it out of my city. The war chose to come here and turn our city into a kind of hell. But it hasn't changed us into devils. We want a city where all kinds of people live together in peace. We've got no time for flag-waving and talk about

racial purification. Most of the people I know and work
with are good brave people who want nothing more
than peace. And so do the people of Dower. That's why
I wear this white dove – for peace.

Uproar. Dr JAMESON slowly rises and quiets the crowd.

JAMESON: I'm sorry, Mr Mayor, but I do think that's
exactly the kind of defeatist talk we can do without.

THUG TWO: She's half a Gnasher!

Boos.

THUG ONE: Get back to your hospital.

MAYOR: If you'd like to add anything, Dr Jameson?

JAMESON: (*Rising.*) Yes, I think I would. Since this press
conference has become a public meeting I would like
to say that the good brave people of Arden do want
something more than peace. They want justice!

Cheers.

MOUTH: They do. And they want leadership! Strong
leadership!

Cheers.

I nominate Dr Jameson to be Governor of this city.

Big cheers.

THUGS: Jameson! Jameson! Jameson!

JAMESON: (*Modestly.*) We already have a leader.

MAYOR: I shall continue to negotiate.

Boos.

JAMESON: My friends, this is our own city, our
beautiful city. Anyone who seeks to destroy it must
reckon with us – the courageous people of Arden.

Big cheers.

MOUTH: All those in favour of Dr Jameson as Governor of this city, as long as the emergency lasts?

Nearly all the people put up their hands.

INGRID: All those against?

INGRID and a few others put up their hands. MAYOR puts his up at first, then, realising he's in a minority, puts it down.

WE'LL BE GOING
(an old super-patriotic Ardenian song)

JAMESON / MOUTH / THUGS / ALL: (*Sing.*)
We'll be going
Where blood is flowing
And bayonets flash in the sun
We're all willing
To do some killing
When there's a job to be done
Where guns are loading
And bombs exploding
That's where we bravely will stand
You'll find us slaughtering
Hanging, drawing and quartering
All for the love of our land
For the love
Of our beautiful land!

Cheers – from those who haven't slunk away from this appalling rally.

TEACHER: No windows.

MOUTH: Yes ha ha. I couldn't give you notice but these two distinguished people are international observers. From the United Nations. And they want to report on the situation in Arden.

TEACHER: We try to keep the school running. There's no heating, so we close down in winter. The streets round here are favourites with the snipers in the hills. So you never know who's going to turn up. Me, I'm the only teacher today.

MELANIE: That's cos you're bullet-proof.

VISITOR ONE: Yes, we'd like to hear from the children.

LUCY: Esther did a great history essay.

TEACHER: Let's hear it, Esther.

ESTHER: It's about a siege in the Middle Ages. Er, this is it.

'They're out there, all the time, watching and waiting. I can't do anything without thinking of them. At night they drink mulled ale, shouting and singing until my head throbs and aches. In the daytime they catapult terrible things over our walls. Yesterday they catapulted a dead horse – I can still see its carcass, battered and bloody, buzzing with dead flies. The day before it was a bundle of black rats. Two servants have died since then. We fear the plague is upon us. There is no escape. We are surrounded. Like frightened rabbits we hide in our warren, while the foxes sniff at our door. How long will the food last? I keep a small dagger with me all the time…'

[*By Esther Bintliff, Durham.*]

MOUTH: Very good indeed Esther. Not exactly cheerful, but very good.

ELLI: My little cousin Dina dictated a letter to me. She said she wanted it sent to the world. It says: 'My name is Dina and I am four years old. I would like to send a message to those shooting from the hills. "Go home to your own children and never come back to Arden." I want peace to come so we can all sleep in our own homes, not in cellars with the spiders and the mice. I wish this war would stop so that I can go again to visit my grandma in her house. She always has a bowl of fruit.'

[*Based on a letter by Dijana, aged four, from Sarajevo.*]

MOUTH: I wonder what you children read? There is an excellent history of the people of Arden – City of Glory – published by the Church of Purity. That'll help you feel proud of your heritage.

TEACHER: We did try to read that book. But we have all races and religions in this school – it wasn't appropriate.

MOUTH: Even if you have Doweranian children in your school, they should be taught to understand the proud heritage of our city.

VISITOR TWO: Do the children write their own poetry? I teach a poetry class in Geneva.

LUCY: You want to hear Karl's poem.

KARL: O God, here goes. (*Reads.*) *Ben and His Shrapnel.*

On the second day of the second week
Ben handed me his yellow Spiderman lunch-box
I let it drop on the floor
It was twenty times heavier than I expected
It just missed my trainers
What have you got for lunch, Ben?
Rockburgers?

Ben smiled and opened his Spiderman lunch-box.
It was full of shrapnel.
Shining jabs of metal with zig-zag teeth,
Every piece as heavy as a chair.

Ben's my best friend,
He let me choose a bit of shrapnel.
Then the whole class crowded round us:
Come on, Ben, give us a little one.
Come on, Ben, I'll be your best friend!
But he shook his head and closed the Spiderman lid.

By the fourth day of the fourth week
The shrapnel craze was at its hottest.
Even the smallest kid
Had a desk full of metal lumps.
There weren't many windows left in our school
And we all wore coats and gloves all day.

By the fifth day of the fifth week
There was so much shrapnel in every street
It wasn't worth picking up.
We ran and dodged along to school
Carrying blankets, curtains,
Anything to wrap ourselves up in.
It was February and the wind was white with ice
And there were two craters in the playground
And some walls had collapsed.
There were no windows left at all
And Ben didn't come to school any more.

MOUTH: (*To TEACHER*.) It's a funny thing, but your
pupils do seem to turn out very defeatist versions of
the truth. They don't seem to understand what the
people of Arden are fighting for.

ARLO: We understand. This is a war with no meaning
and no end.

MOUTH: And what's your name?

ARLO: Arlo Swados.

THUG ONE writes it down.

MOUTH: And how old are you, Mr Swados?

ARLO: Nearly sixteen.

MOUTH: Good. Sixteen – that's when you'll be called for military service.

ARLO: That's what they tell me.

MOUTH: You'd better learn fast in the Army.

ARLO: Would I be safer if I joined the Church of Purity?

THUG ONE: Watch it, Swados. You'll end up in the Majestic.

VISITOR TWO: What's the Majestic?

MOUTH: The old Majestic cinema. We have no electricity now. It's used as a reception centre.

KARL: We call it the Horrordrome.

VISITOR TWO: Why?

KARL: That's where they question prisoners.

MOUTH: The city's awash with rumours, of course.

ANDREA: I was in the waiting room at the Horrordrome. With my mother. They keep a big glass jar up on a shelf in there. It's full of people's tongues. Tongues all pickled.

TEACHER: For God's sake, Andrea.

MOUTH: Yes, that'll do – Andrea.

THUG ONE: (*Writing down her name.*) Andrea.

VISITOR ONE: (*To TEACHER.*) Thank you so much. Your pupils have been very eloquent. You see we do want to try to experience what the people of Arden are experiencing.

TEACHER: I'm afraid you're missing an essential part of the Arden experience.

VISITOR ONE: What's that?

TEACHER: To experience what we're experiencing – get yourself out of here on the next plane. Fly home. Collect your mother and your wife and your children. Bring them back here. Teach them to queue for bread and water and dodge bullets. Have them come here and watch them try to live here and watch them die here. Then you'll understand the experience.

VISITOR ONE: Yes, well thank you.

VISITORS exit. MOUTH pauses with THUG ONE.

MOUTH: (*To THUG ONE.*) All right. I know that teacher's name.

Exit MOUTH and THUG ONE. TEACHER and PUPILS clear classroom.

SCENE SEVEN

BIRTHDAY PLANS

The Swados family house. SALLY and INGRID enter and sit on the table. SALLY produces an apple.

SALLY: Share it with you.

INGRID: Thanks. (*Takes a bite, hands it back.*) Sally, we've got to get serious. Only two weeks till the twins' birthday.

SALLY: I wish they were going to be six instead of gun age.

INGRID: We've got to get the other kids organised. Cards, presents, a party.

SALLY: How the hell can we give them a birthday cake? No flour. No sugar.

INGRID: You know that airline pilot who took me out last week?

SALLY: The Italian with a nicotine moustache?

INGRID: He gave me three presents. (*Producing bags out of her shoulder bag.*) Flour. Sugar. Marzipan.

SALLY: Marzipan! Ingrid, you're a saint.

INGRID: Saints don't get marzipan.

Enter the kids from school — minus BETSY and ARLO. LUCY, KARL, ELLI with their friends JAMES, MELANIE and GABY.

SALLY: Where are the twins?

LUCY: Down the Stargate Club.

SALLY: We're going to make them the greatest birthday cake ever seen in Arden. And it's thanks to Ingrid! Flour! Sugar! Marzipan!

Cheers.

KARL: We can't just give em cake. Arlo's in such a bad way since Dad was killed. We've got to cheer him up.

LUCY: A party'll do the trick!

ELLI: I'll be a clown and turn cartwheels.

KARL: Big deal.

GABY: I bet I can get that band plays down the Stargate.

SALLY: We'll bop till we drop.

KARL: That won't take long if we don't have any food.

ELLI: Bit of tinned fruit. Peanut butter sandwiches.

MELANIE: Crisps.

JAMES: Jelly and chocolate.

INGRID: Happy dreams.

JAMES: Birthday presents.

LUCY: We got no money.

ELLI: Nothing in the shops.

SALLY: We can make things for the twins.

KARL: I'd knit a sweater if I had some wool. If I knew how to knit.

ELLI: We can write poems for them.

GABY: That's it. Anyone can write a poem.

IT'S THE LOVING THAT MATTERS

GABY: (*Sings.*)
    We wrote this poem because it's your birthday
    We wrote it because of what we want to say
    And even if they drop a bomb
    This poem's going to carry on
    And even if the words sound wrong
    At least we made you up a birthday song
                  [*From Hampstead Shool impro*]

    It's the loving that matters
    In a time of hate
    It's the feeling that matters
    And we all feel great

> You're a little bit wild
> And you're certainly weird
> But we celebrate the day when you first appeared
> Cos it's the loving that matters
> In a time of hate
> It's the feeling that matters
> And we all feel great –
> Happy birthday – Betsy and Arlo –
>
> C'mon everybody!

ALL: (*Sing.*)

> It's the loving that matters
> In a time of hate
> It's the feeling that matters
> And we all feel great
> You're a little bit wild
> And you're certainly weird
> But we celebrate the day when you first appeared
> Cos it's the loving that matters
> In a time of hate
> It's the feeling that matters
> And we all feel great –
> Happy birthday – Betsy and Arlo –
> Happy birthday!

SALLY: (*To INGRID.*) Come on, let's get this cake started.

Exit SALLY and INGRID.

MELANIE: Well I reckon we should put all our money on the table and divvy it out and then go down the market and each buy something for the twins.

ELLI: I know what they want. Bikes.

LUCY: Here's my life savings!

SCENE SIX

THE OPEN SCHOOL

Lower Stage. Enter TEACHER with file, followed by PUPILS. These include the Swados kids, BETSY, ARLO, LUCY, KARL and ELLI as well as JAMES, MELANIE and GABY, ESTHER, an intelligent teenager and ANDREA, who is about 12.

TEACHER: (*Who is energetic but and brave, but also highly strung and no wonder.*) All right, everybody. Settle down. I'm the only teacher who made it through the crossfire this morning –

Cheers.

– because I'm totally bullet-proof. So it's just one class in the Open School today.

BETSY: We got to work with the little kids again?

TEACHER: All of us together. Can you deal with that Betsy?

BETSY: Watch me.

A knock at the door.

TEACHER: Come in.

Enter Revd MOUTH with two VISITORS and, keeping in the background, THUG ONE. PUPILS stand.

MOUTH: Good morning and sit you down.

PUPILS: Good morning.

TEACHER motions them to sit.

MOUTH: Excuse this rather sudden surprise visit –

TEACHER: Everyone's welcome to the Open School.

MOUTH: The Open School?

ALL the Swados kids and friends look in pockets and bags and make a small pile of change. One five pound note from GABY, who counts the money.

GABY: Nine pounds 84p.

LUCY: Won't buy much of a bike.

KARL: We'll have to nick something.

ELLI: Stealing's wrong.

MELANIE: It's a special occasion.

KARL: We're not asking you to do it. You know that dense woman with all the cats down the end of the road? She's got jewellery in her kitchen drawer. I saw it.

MELANIE: I could sort of distract her. Talk to her about cats.

KARL: I nip in and out with a necklace or two.

MELANIE: Zip down the market.

KARL: (*Acting it out.*) What'll you give us on this bracelet?

MELANIE: (*As Street Trader.*) You stole that, didn't you?

KARL: Doesn't affect you. Give us thirty quid for it.

MELANIE: No, a tenner.

KARL: Come on, that's silly stuff.

MELANIE: All right, twelve.

KARL: Bullshit.

MELANIE: Fifteen quid, that's my stopper.

KARL: Fifteen quid! Spend it on a whole bunch of dodgy presents.

GABY: Any of that and I take my note out of the kitty.
No nicking.

JAMES: There's some heavy dudes down the market.
Face it, we need twice the money to get much more
than a bar of second-hand soap.

LUCY: Come on – divvy up the cash. Market's open.

Money's divided and all exit.

SCENE EIGHT

MOONCRATER MARKET

*The market in a square. STALLHOLDERS bring on stalls. Some
may be on wheels, some may be very simple tables. Mooncrater
Market is the opposite of the colourful, overflowing markets of – say
– France. A typical stall might be a plain table with a few carrots
and the odd knitted hat for a child spread on an old newspaper.
Many of the stalls are mixed with all sorts of goods: soap, matches,
lighters, pepper, cotton, old shoes, stolen clothes, salt, a little coffee,
second-hand silverware and tools. Bartering is welcome. A sign says
MOONCRATER MARKET in big bright letters. The crump of shells in
the distance. STALLHOLDERS tend to wear leather jackets either
brown or black, cowboy boots. Stubble for the blokes. MYSTICAL
MARIGOLD, who wears a white dove, has a fortune teller stall
and there is a little group of DRUGPUSHERS including JESSIE
Nola, whom we meet later. At the centre of the square is a raised
platform with a statue of a heroic Arden statesman, hand upraised
in oratory.*

THUGS ONE and TWO are on patrol in the market, quietly.

MOONCRATER MARKET

STALLHOLDERS: (*Sing.*) Mooncrater Market
Everyone's your sister

And brother
Mooncrater Market
For a little bit of this
And that and the other
Mooncrater Market
You'll find something to fit
It's not a scam, Sam,
It's all legit
Once seen
Can't be forgotten
The prices high
The food rotten
So bring your stroller
Or your Roller
And park it
Slap in the middle of
Mooncrater Market!

KNIFESELLER: (*Sings.*)
Knives and forks and spoons and such
They're a little bit crap but they don't cost much!

MILKSELLER: (*Sings.*)
Powdered milk
Keep the baby happy
Powdered milk
Smells sweet in the nappy

MYSTICAL MARIGOLD: (*Sings.*)
What is your future?
Want your fortune told?
There's nobody but Mystical Marigold

MUSTARDSELLER: (*Sings.*)
French mustard!

CUSTARDSELLER: (*Sings.*)
English custard!

PASSPORTSELLER: (*Sings.*)
    We got passports
    Documents of allsorts

TICKETSELLER: (*Sings.*)
    Buy a lucky ticket
    And stick it in the bucket
    We may pick it
    In the draw for
    A bottle of fine Rhine wine!

VEGETABLESELLER: (*Sings.*)
    Healthy diet if you like to go jogging
    Individual carrots is what I'm flogging

MAGAZINESELLER: (*Sings.*)
    Glossy magazine
    Not obscene but erotic

MEDICINESELLER: (*Sings.*)
    Kill off your germs
    With some anti-biotic

WEAPONSELLER: (*Sings.*)
    I got bullets
    I got blades
    I got pistols and
    Hand grenades

DRUGPUSHERS: (*Sings.*)
    You want weed?
    You like E?
    You on crack?
    See me.
    Up or down
    No more sadness
    My drugs
    Are badnessss!!

STALLHOLDERS: (*Sing.*)
>If you can't see it on the counter
>Doesn't mean we don't stock it
>It could hop from under the counter
>To your inside pocket –
>Check it, check it, check it –
>
>Mooncrater Market
>Everyone's your sister
>And brother
>Mooncrater Market
>For a little bit of this
>And that and the other
>Mooncrater Market
>You'll find something to fit
>It's not a scam, Sam,
>It's all legit
>Once seen
>Can't be forgotten
>The prices high
>The food rotten
>So bring your stroller
>Or your Roller
>And park it
>Slap in the middle of
>Mooncrater Market!

*GABY, LUCY, KARL, JAMES, MELANIE and ELLI come
into the market and start looking around. GABY and LUCY
stop by the MILKSELLER's stall, who like most stallholders,
sells anything he can get his hands on.*

MILKSELLER: (*Sings.*)
>Powdered milk
>Keep the baby happy –

LUCY: Do we look like we got babies? Well then, we're
looking for birthday presents.

MILKSELLER: (*Demonstrating umbrella.*) Fine umbrella, suit all weathers, I don't want three quid for it, I don't want two quid, I don't even want one quid – ninety pee for a bran new umbrella!

LUCY: (*Whispers.*) It's not bad.

GABY: It's not big enough for one twin, let alone two.

MUSTARDSELLER: Lovely jacket, lady, purest velvet all the way from Morocco.

LUCY: Wouldn't fit a monkey.

CUSTARDSELLER: Belgian chocolate, best quality.

GABY: It's fattening.

CUSTARDSELLER: No calories in this chocolate.

GABY: That's all right, we got no money.

THUG ONE: (*Coming over.*) You selling chocolate for no sweet coupons?

CUSTARDSELLER: (*Drops bar of chocolate, kicks it under the stall.*) What chocolate? I sell custard, don't I?

THUG ONE: (*Removing chocolate.*) That's fine then.

KARL: (*To JAMES.*) I know what, we could get the twins a little pick-me-up.

JAMES: What you mean?

KARL: Sure. (*Goes to DRUGPUSHER.*) Hey, Andy, how's the business?

DRUGPUSHER: Still afloat, Karl boy. I'm giving out a lot of comfort these days. Some go for sex and some lean on God, but I'm the only real source of hope these days.

KARL: Any top grade dope?

JAMES: For a birthday present.

DRUGPUSHER: Wicked. Now this little packet —

GABY: (*Getting between DRUGPUSHER and KARL.*) Deal over. You know what that stuff does to Arlo's head.

KARL: (*Veering off to other stalls with JAMES.*) I'm not buying the twins bloody galoshes.

MELANIE and ELLI are nervously approaching MYSTICAL MARIGOLD.

MYSTICAL MARIGOLD: Hello, sit down.

MELANIE: Do we cross your palm with silver?

MYSTICAL MARIGOLD: What do you want, my child?

ELLI: Well I have this brother and sister and they're twins and they're going to be sixteen and we thought as a present we could get their fortunes told and tell them when the siege is going to end too.

MELANIE: Can you do that?

MYSTICAL MARIGOLD: I used to look into people's faces and there I would see what they wanted to know, and I told them what they wanted to know and made them believe it by reading their palms or staring into my crystal ball. But now that we are trapped in the dark crystal ball of this city, I can see nothing in their faces. I can tell you nothing.

The MAYOR has entered and approached MYSTICAL MARIGOLD as ELLI and MELANIE drift away, disappointed.

MAYOR: How's the futures business, Marigold?

MYSTIC MARIGOLD: I'm no use to the people any more, Carlos. They're turning away from me.

MAYOR: I know the feeling.

GABY: (*To the KIDS.*) Come on, let's get home and look at the presents.

GABY exits along with KARL, JAMES, MELANIE, LUCY and ELLI.

WEAPONSELLER: Hey? Mr Leman. You meant to be the Mayor, right? I'm being hassled day and night by these heavies –

TICKETSELLER: Me too, and you don't know if they're cops or gangsters –

WEAPONSELLER: – All the same, they're asking protection money, insurance they call it –

TICKETSELLER: And you're meant to be protecting us –

MAYOR: You must understand these are very difficult times –

MAGAZINESELLER: And very dodgy people in charge of this city, if you ask me.

The Revd MOUTH has entered with Dr JAMESON. They stand beside the heroic statue. MOUTH coughs to draw attention. INGRID, who has entered and started inspecting stalls, turns and listens.

MOUTH: There comes a time when it is necessary to speak out. There stands our Mayor, Mr Carlos Leman. He has led us to the brink of disaster. He has been slow, indecisive and apathetic. He can't govern, he can't plan, he can't fight. The heroic people of Arden are dying of starvation because of his incompetence.

MAYOR: I'm conducting international negotiations –

JAMESON: Carlos, you're a good husband and an excellent father. But you're much too nice a man to be a leader.

For a time you lulled us to sleep with fairy tales of United Nations help. But now the fairy tale is over and your children have grown up. The people of Arden say to you now – step aside, out of the way! Our League of New Justice is the only hope of the people.

MOUTH: Step aside – make way for the People! Make way for the League of New Justice and Governor Jameson – the voice of the future!

Shouts of affirmation from the crowd. THUG ONE steps up to MAYOR and takes him by the arm.

THUG ONE: Perhaps you'll come this way, sir? For your own protection.

People shout and jeer at the MAYOR as he is led off. Suddenly INGRID speaks out.

INGRID: (*To the crowd.*) Do you have any idea who you're handing power to? This man is an arms smuggler and a gangster.

THINK

(*Sings backed by a few voices.*) Think
Look around you
Look around your home
Look around your school
Look around your town
Look around your country and your continent too
Look around the world
And think

What's going down?
Who's ruling who?
Who's hurting who?
Who's torturing who?

Who's the jailer, who's the prisoner?
Just think

What's going down?
Who's got the power?
Who's got the property?
Who's got the land?
Who's got the money?
Hey think

What's going down?
Who's got the power of prison in their hand?
Who's got your life and death at their command?
Who's got the power to send you out to war?
How did they get that power?
Did we give it?
Did they grab it?
How long, how long, how long, how long?
Come on and think
Think and then
Act.

JAMESON: Ever since you arrived in this city you've been preaching pacifism and surrender to the bravest people in the world. They're all sick of your cowardly talk. Take her away. Arden has no time for traitors.

INGRID: (*Walking towards JAMESON.*) You've no authority in this city.

THUG TWO: Stand back, lady.

INGRID walks on. THUG TWO draws a pistol.

I warned you.

Blackout. Surge of the music but not the singing of the superpatriotic song 'We'll Be Going'.

SCENE NINE

THE STARGATE CLUB

On Upper Stage, a band setting up. A sign announces THE STARGATE CLUB. *LUCY, KARL and ELLI sit round table discussing their shopping expedition.*

LUCY: It's hopeless.

KARL: Nothing we could afford.

LUCY: Nothing worth buying.

KARL: Gaby and co. didn't do any better. Just a gang of crooks down the market.

LUCY: What's up, Elli?

ELLI: Oh. I was thinking about that bomb site behind our house.

KARL: It's all bust up bricks and plaster and stuff.

ELLI: I was thinking – it wouldn't cost much. Be a lot of work.

LUCY: What're you on about Elli?

ELLI: We could make that patch into a kind of a garden. As a birthday present for the twins. Lots of people would help.

LUCY: Would plants grow there?

KARL: Maybe some.

ELLI: They wouldn't be ready in time – not real plants. We'd make them – trees and flowers and animals too. Make 'em out of old wood cut up and painted up and nailed together – like statues.

LUCY: We could make statues too. Statues of people the twins like – like John Travolta and Anne Frank and Jarvis Cocker.

KARL: I'd like to be in charge of making the animals – making tigers and elephants and wombats and stuff.

LUCY: Birds too –

ELLI: Sun, moon and stars.

KARL: We only got a couple of weeks.

LUCY: Better get started recruiting people.

ELLI: Let's go.

As they're going out, BETSY and ARLO are coming in.

ARLO: What you doing in the Stargate?

LUCY: Oh, you know – just plotting mighty plots.

Exit LUCY, ELLI and KARL. BETSY and ARLO sit down.

BETSY: Right, Arlo, what is it?

ARLO: You know I've been getting these messages? From High Command?

BETSY: Your voices, yes. Those pills always spark them off.

ARLO: No. They're true messages, Betsy.

BETSY: What are they saying?

ARLO: I've got to get out of Arden.

BETSY: Nobody gets out of Arden. Tell your voices there's a siege.

ARLO: High Command says I've got to escape. Before our birthday.

BETSY: So that you'll miss being called up into the Army?

ARLO: You've got it. It's strict orders. I'm not allowed to kill anyone. It's been decided.

BETSY: What about me? I don't have to join the Army, but I'll be in the home defence militia. I'll have to carry a gun.

ARLO: Oh no. You're coming with me.

BETSY: Well I wouldn't let you go alone, kid. But how'd we get out?

ARLO: There are ways and means. You have to bribe the right man.

BETSY: Your voices told you that?

ARLO: I knew that anyway. People do get out, now and then. Across the river. But we mustn't tell anyone.

BETSY: Not even Mum?

ARLO: She wouldn't let us risk it.

BETSY: It's one hell of a chance. But if we stay I don't think you'd survive a week in the Army.

ARLO: Right... Look. There's a lot to be fixed. We'll have to leave it till the night before our birthday.

BETSY: And then we cross the river? Listen...

BETSY and ARLO keep talking silently to each other as the STARGATE BAND goes into the number which closes Act One.

A NEW FACE IN A NEW PLACE

STARGATE BAND: (*Sing.*)
Don't know how the future's going to smell

It could be Heaven and it may be Hell
All I know is that I need some space
To be a new face
In a new place

I'm not nervous of the days ahead
I may survive I'll maybe end up dead
All I know is I'm a hopeless case
Without a new face
In a new place

New face
Kind of calm and wise
New face
With wide open eyes
New face
Under new skies
New face
With wide open eyes

Don't know how the story's going to end
I could be king or left without a friend
I could be full of shit or full of grace
Like a new face
In a new place.

End of Act One.

ACT TWO

SCENE ONE

LEAVING NOW

Inside a Church.

An altar with candelabra, silver goblet, cross etc. Rev MOUTH, the priest who acts as right-hand man to the gang-leader Dr JAMESON, is officiating at the end of a service. CONGREGATION, many of them women with scarves. Stained glass window effect if possible. If the actor playing MOUTH is not a strong singer it is possible to have another SINGER to sing his lines while MOUTH looks on approvingly. FEATHERS, who joins in as a soloist, is a comparatively brightly dressed woman who is MOUTH's mistress. During the Psalm, BETSY and ALDO enter and join the congregation.

23rd PSALM

MOUTH: (*Chants.*) Yea. Though I walk through the valley

CONGREGATION: Though I walk through the valley

MOUTH: The valley of the shadow of death

CONGREGATION: Though I walk through the valley
The valley of the shadow of death

MOUTH: I will fear no evil

CONGREGATION: I will fear no evil

MOUTH / CONGREGATION:
Though I walk through the valley
Of the shadow of death
I will fear no evil
I will fear no evil

MOUTH: For thou art with me

CONGREGATION: Thou art with me

MOUTH: Thy rod and thy staff they comfort me.

FEATHERS: (*As soloist.*)
Thou preparedst a table before me
In the presence of mine enemies;
Thou anointest my head with oil;
My cup runneth over.

MOUTH: Surely goodness and mercy shall follow me

CONGREGATION: Goodness and mercy shall follow me

MOUTH: All the days of my life

CONGREGATION: All the days of my life

MOUTH / CONGREGATION:
And I will dwell in the house of the Lord
For ever
And I will dwell in the house of the Lord
For ever.
Amen.

MOUTH makes sign of the Cross. CONGREGATION begin to disperse, whispering together. But BETSY and ARLO remain. FEATHERS approaches MOUTH.

FEATHERS: Am I cooking your dinner tonight, Oliver?

MOUTH: How long are you free for, Feathers?

FEATHERS: Till four in the morning. My old man's on the graveyard shift.

MOUTH: Drop round at eight. I've got the meat.

Sees the TWINS still hanging around.

Now buzz off to the vestry. (*More loudly.*) And bless you, my daughter.

Exit FEATHERS.

Approach, my young friends.

BETSY and ARLO walk up to him. They have met before and the encounter is strained.

BETSY: This is confidential.

MOUTH: Of course. You have a spiritual problem?

BETSY: Nope. A business proposition.

MOUTH: This is a church, my child.

BETSY: This is cash, father.

MOUTH: You have my undivided attention.

ARLO: What it is, we've got to cross the river.

MOUTH: That's against the law.

ARLO: I've got my orders. From the High Command.

MOUTH: There's no such –

BETSY: Arlo hears voices –

ARLO: (*Laughs.*) Yes, like Joan of Arc. We've got to cross the river.

MOUTH: You're planning to desert your native town? Maybe you'd betray us? I know you two. You're from the Swados family and they've always been a slippery bunch.

BETSY: We've never been religious bigots or racists if that's what you mean.

ARLO: Don't argue. High Command says we mustn't argue.

MOUTH: Then High Command's got its head screwed on. You need guidance.

BETSY: You can stuff it.

MOUTH: My dear Miss Swados. In order to reach the river, you will have to walk three miles over the water-meadows. And those fields are planted with thousands of little landmines. Tripwire mines, bounding mines –

ARLO: What's a bounding mine?

MOUTH: Jumps up before it explodes. Belly height for an adult, face height for a child. But most mines just sit there in the grass like tortoises. Very efficient – made in England. Step on one and you're dogmeat from the waist down.

BETSY: What comes after the minefields?

MOUTH: You have to cross the border fence, on which you might easily find yourself impaled till the snipers, in their mercy, finish you off. If you get over the fence, you dodge through Polecat Wood. Then you'll need a boat to carry you downstream and over the river onto neutral ground.

BETSY: We need guidance.

MOUTH: It'll cost you five hundred, or would you rather I stuffed it?

BETSY: I was told three hundred.

MOUTH: You're a bad-mannered girl. I charge extra for that.

ARLO: You'll see us through?

MOUTH: My boys will show you how to thread the minefield. How to hop the fence. Where to find the boat. But you go it alone.

BETSY: (*Who has been counting money, hands over a bunch of notes.*) There you are.

MOUTH: Call me Father.

ARLO: You're not our father. No. (*Hitting his chest.*) My father's in here. You can't steal my father – (*About to attack MOUTH.*)

BETSY: (*Restraining ARLO.*) He's trying to help us, Arlo. High Command says not to argue.

MOUTH: That's right, boy, I'm doing my best for you.

ARLO: Sorry, sorry…

BETSY: When can we start?

MOUTH: Right away, my children. May God go with you.

THUGS ONE and TWO emerge from behind altar.

THUG ONE: This way, kids.

THUG TWO: Move it.

BETSY and ARLO follow THUGS out. MOUTH produces a whisky bottle from underneath altar-cloth. Pours himself a large one in silver goblet. Sips.

MOUTH: Steak and chips, that's what I fancy tonight. Steak and chips with little burnt onions and gravy. And Feathers, of course. Feathers! High Command calling!

Exit MOUTH.

Fade on Church. Remove altar.

SCENE TWO

THE POWTEX ARMS FAIR

On the Upper Stage. A bar. Facing us, leaning on it, MEN in suits. Among them, a big Arms DEALER with a SECRETARY, talking with Doweranian COLONEL from Act One Scene Two. A big sign proclaims POWTEX ARMS FAIR. *Posters for various guns, mines, shells etc on the front of the bar. A couple of BARWAITERS busily supplying drinks. A couple of armed SECURITY GUARDS. During the song, singers freeze into posed handshakes and smiles lit by flash cameras.*

MEN IN WHITE SHIRTS

ALL: (*Sing.*) Men in white shirts.
    Men in dark suits.
    Men shaking hands.
    Men smiling smiles.

    Men in white shirts.
    Men in dark suits.
    Signing their names.
    Making their deals...

    Have another Scotch.
    This is the wife.
    Fabulous watch!
    This is the life.

    Men in white shirts,
    Men in dark suits.
    Men shaking hands.
    Men smiling smiles.

DEALER: Just off the record, Colonel, how much longer can Arden hold out?

COLONEL: They're an obstinate bunch. But we've got them in a stranglehold.

DEALER: What's on your shopping list this year?

SECRETARY taking notes.

COLONEL: Mainly the same order – Kalashnikovs, MP-5 sub-machine guns, G3 sniper rifles, landmines. And

we'd like to go for some cluster bombs. And maybe
napalm. Maybe.

DEALER: We can't send 'em direct to Dower any more.

COLONEL: Ghastly United Nations embargos, eh?

DEALER: No probs. We've got a company called Triple-
T-X. We send everything to you via the Middle East.
Shall we talk quantity?

COLONEL: Hang on.

*Enter JAMESON casually. JAMESON obviously knows both
COLONEL and DEALER.*

DEALER: (*Shaking hands.*) Dr Jameson, I presume.

JAMESON: Fancy meeting you here, Colonel.

COLONEL: You know how it is. If we didn't buy the
odd water pistol, a lot of people would lose their jobs.

JAMESON: Working hard to reduce unemployment.
(*Raises glass.*) Cheers, Colonel Gnasher.

COLONEL: Cheers, Doctor Mudhead. Are you enjoying
the siege these days?

JAMESON: (*Smiling.*) Well, I'm very fully employed.

COLONEL: We can chat later. I'd better get my
shopping done first.

JAMESON: (*To DEALER.*) I'll have whatever the
Colonel's having.

SECRETARY: Shall I take you to the Catalogue and
Order Tent, sir?

*COLONEL nods, smiles and follows SECRETARY out.
DEALER and JAMESON drink together.*

JAMESON: What are those Doweranian characters up
to?

DEALER: It's like this – yes, double Scotch, thanks
Doctor.

ALL: (*Sing.*) Men in white shirts.
Men in dark suits.
Signing their names.
Making their deals.

Men in white shirts.
Men in dark suits.
Ruling the world,
Ruling the world.

SCENE THREE

THE MINEFIELD

Evening. Getting dark.

*Enter, upstage right, THUGS ONE and TWO, followed by BETSY
and ARLO with backpacks. THUGS stop suddenly and turn to
TWINS.*

THUG ONE: Here it is then.

BETSY: This is where the minefields start?

THUG ONE: All the way to the border fence.

THUG TWO: Scattered all over, hid in the grass.

THUG ONE: Hundreds and thousands of little mines.

ARLO: How we going to get through?

THUG ONE: It's a maze. But this'll take you through.

*THUG ONE bends down, picks up the end of a long piece
of ribbon.*

ARLO: That's just a bit of ribbon.

THUG TWO: Take it. Hang on to it.

THUG ONE: Lose the ribbon, lose your legs. No. Just follow it along, winding in and out. It should lead you round the maze, across the fields, all the way to a bit of the border fence where the current's switched off. With any luck. Then you hop the fence, through Polecat Woods and there'll be a little boat in the river, stuck under the willows. Jump in, take it downstream for about a mile, then out and up the other side of the river.

THUG TWO: And you'll be in neutral bloody territory. And very nice too. You won't have to lay down your life for your own people, will you?

ARLO: I've been told I mustn't. By the High Command.

THUG ONE: That's all right then. Good luck. Just one thing. You'll need a torch.

He hands over an electric torch.

ARLO: Oh thanks.

THUG ONE: That'll be thirty.

BETSY: (*Paying.*) Batteries included?

THUG ONE: Oh yeah. On your way. Just hope some bloody rabbit hasn't hopped in and swallowed your ribbon. Come on, mate.

Exit THUGS, upstage right.

BETSY: Get behind me, Arlo. Look, take the ribbon like me. Left hand. Make a circle round it with your thumb and forefinger. Don't pull on it. Can't risk breaking it.

ARLO: Follow the ribbon, Betsy. I'll follow you.

The TWINS walk slowly, following the ribbon, which takes them in a winding course. Darker and darker. BETSY uses her torch.

Music. Two rifle shots. The TWINS drop, pause, get up and continue.

What's that up ahead?

BETSY shines her torch briefly. There is a high security fence composed of massed actors. She switches off the torch.

BETSY: Must be the border fence. No more talking. We'll have to climb over in the dark. There'll be snipers. Coats off and over.

In deadly silence but for the sound of wind and wire creaking, the TWINS place their coats over the fence to protect them from barbed wire and help each other to climb up and over. TWINS drop to the other side of the fence. They recover.

Through the wood and down to the river. Come on.

Exit TWINS upstage left.

SCENE FOUR

PARTY TIME ONE

The Swados home.

Getting ready for the TWINS' 16th birthday party. SALLY, LUCY, KARL, ELLI, GABY, JAMES and MELANIE. SALLY, who wears a mourning band on her arm, is preparing a big birthday cake very carefully. GABY and LUCY are working on costumes. LUCY in a new, shiny and rather tight party costume. KARL, reluctantly, is helping ELLI, JAMES and MELANIE painting large flowers, animals etc for the Jungle of Arden.

See introductory note on the Jungle of Arden at the beginning of the final scene and in Production Notes. Music.

KARL: (*Making a face.*) Pigs in space! I got flaming paint on me best jeans.

ELLI: Just do it careful.

MELANIE: Take your time. It looks great.

KARL: It looks crap. What's the point?

GABY puts down the dress she's sewing and comes over. She's in charge of the creation of the jungle and she's not going to let it drop.

GABY: Listen, Karl. What you're doing's important. Part of our big present. For Betsy and Arlo.

KARL: Big present! Big heap of crap!

GABY: Come on, be a cheerful little dung-beetle. No. Look. See that bomb site out there. Just rubble and brick-dust and a couple of burned-out cars!

KARL: Yeah. Horrible.

GABY: Well, it won't be. Not when we finished with it. We're going to make bloody great daisies and roses and dahlias and dogs and camels and snakes and elephants and funny sort of statues of Pele and Mickey Mouse and Madonna and The Beatles and we're going to paint them every colour paint there is in the Universe and we're going to fix up seven suns and twenty-one moons and a zillion stars and we'll build palm-trees and fir trees and oak-trees and monkey-puzzle trees... And on their birthday morning we'll lead Betsy and Arlo blindfold out into the middle of that shining great jungle and we'll take off their blindfolds – and they'll think they've died and gone to heaven.

MELANIE: And then what?

LUCY: I'll do my Birthday Dance. And then we'll party!

ALL: Party!

LUCY: Yeah we'll party!

LUCY: PARTY!

ALL: PARTY!

LUCY: COS IT'LL BE PARTY TIME!

ALL: PARTY TIME!

GABY: That's a fantastic dress, Lucy, but it's going to split.

LUCY: It's fine till I try to move.

MELANIE: Bit tight round the back.

ELLI: Who's going to look at your back? Where's Mum?

KARL: Trying to find out what happened to Ingrid.

JAMES: Your Mum's great. Scared of nothing.

LUCY: She lost Dad. She's got nothing to lose.

ELLI: She got us. She got us.

ELLI's going to cry, so LUCY hugs her.

LUCY: Course she got us.

MELANIE: She'll be home soon.

GABY: Hey, come on, Karl. Thought you were meant to be giving a hand.

KARL: (*Stands up, notebook in hand.*) You said we was going to put on a sort of birthday show in the jungle? Yeah?

GABY: Yeah.

KARL: Well, I just wrote a poem thing for the birthday show. Probably crap. I've not done Betsy's yet. But I wrote this one for Arlo. That's why I call it: *My Big Brother's Birthday.*

Music under the poem.

I got this old white shoe-box
And some runny glue and pink ribbon
Some waxy crayons
And twigs off a tree for candles
And I made you a birthday cake.

You lumbered in like a birthday bear
And gave me your favourite grin.
You said: What an ultimate cake!
It's too excellent to eat.

I said: You've got to guess what's inside the cake.
You guessed – one million pounds.
You guessed – a solid gold helicopter.
You guessed – the cast of Baywatch.
Wrong!

You took ages to open it
With your long strong fingers.
When you looked inside
You took a deep breath and said Wow!! –

It was all full of pretty feathers.
I said: There's two hundred and forty feathers in there,
I counted every one of them when I collected them.
You can pick them up one by one and drop them
And they'll float fluttering down to the floor.
You can fly them whenever you're feeling sad.

You said: If we've got any runny glue left
I'll stick all two hundred and forty to our shoulders
And we'll fly away together
Up into the thin blue sky that's wrapped around the
        globe
Up into the deep blue gaps between the sizzling stars
We'll fly away together
And explore every island in the universe
Cos we're the Flying Birthday Brothers.

Well, that's it, that's what I wrote down.

GABY leads the others in applause.

MELANIE: That's really good, really good.

JAMES: Great.

LUCY: Not half as great as what James and I got. Here's the birthday song we wrote. Listen. Catch it while it's hot.

LUCY and JAMES, as Betsy and Arlo, take the stage for the birthday song. MELANIE, ELLI and GABY act as their backing singers.

YOU GOT TWINS

LUCY / JAMES (*Sing.*) You got twins
You got trouble
You got twins
Got it double
You got a Cantona kick in your shins – ooh –
You got twins

You got twins
You got Babel
Like you're hit
With a table
And you're jumping right out of your skins – ooh –
You got twins

Twice as nice
If you like the squash
When you're up against the wall
And under the cosh
Twice as nice
Like getting stuck in your zipper
On the chopping block
Done up like a kipper

You got twins
No more quiet
You got twins
You got riot
You got a Vinnie Jones grinding your bones – ooh –
You got twins

You got twins
Call for mammy
Here they come
Double-whammy
And that's how the mayhem begins – ooh –
It's the twins

Singleton kids
Are well pathetic
But twins are megacool
Copasetic
Twins were born
To be bitchin twitchin
If you can't stand the heat
Get out of the kitchen

You got twins
Got a punch up
You got twins
Bring your lunch up
You're surely gonna pay for your sins – ooh –
To the twins

You got twins
You got madness
You got twice
Times the badness
Have your skeleton collected in bins – ooh –
By the twins

Twice as hard
As a security guard
Or the pitbull lurking
In a builder's yard
Twice as nice
When you know how it feels
In a suit of armour full
Of electric eels

You got twins
You got trouble
You got twins
Got it double
You'll find there's only two people who wins – ooh –
That's the twins!

This is an out-and-out song and dance number. Others can join in for other verses. Maybe people appear to do verses dressed as Elvis Twins, Marilyn Monroe Twins, Napoleon Twins – whatever. At the end KARL leads the applause.

GABY: Great. It's going to be fantastic. Right. Back to work. Let's go for a happy bloody ending! Right?

ALL: Right!

SCENE FIVE

SNIPERS ON THE HILLS

Lights up on the hills. A group of four SNIPERS, under the command of a SERGEANT, are watching over the landscape above Polecat Woods and the River. There are sandbags, one mortar, rocks and battered trees. The SNIPERS wear heavy boots, camouflage uniforms. There are heavy green boxes of ammunition. SERGEANT and SNIPER ONE are in charge of the mortar. They are taking a break, eating a late dinner out of tins using spoons. One of them plays a mouth organ or concertina or accordion – some sort of very portable instrument whose volume can be held down and is good to sing along with.

ONE HUNDRED MILES AWAY

SNIPER TWO: (*Sings.*) Cold meat from the tin
    Cold beans from the tin
    I've got a red hot woman
    Loves her bottle of gin

ALL: (*Sing.*) But she's one hundred miles away
    One hundred miles from this horrible town
    And I feel like I want to take my rifle in my arms
    And shoot some bastard down

SNIPER TWO: (*Sings.*) Nothing left to smoke
    Nothing left to eat
    I've got a rock roll woman
    Back in Marzipan street

ALL: (*Sing.*) But she's one hundred miles away
    One hundred miles from this horrible town
    And I feel like I want to take my rifle in my arms
    And shoot some bastard down

SNIPER THREE: Shh. Look. Something moving. Down in the wood.

SERGEANT: Hold it. (*Takes a quick look through binoculars.*) Nothing there. At ease.

SNIPER ONE: (*To SNIPER TWO.*) I want to be in a rock-n-roll band when this lot stops.

SNIPER TWO: You can't even play tambourine.

SNIPER ONE: You don't have to play anything. You just sing a bit and jump about. Like Take That.

SERGEANT: Who?

SNIPERS go into an imitation of a Boy Band.

SNIPER ONE: (*Sings.*) Put me in a Boy Band
    I can strut and pout
    Put me in a Boy Band
    Call us Inside Out
    We won't be no toy band
    We can see the rest off
    Put me in a Boy Band
    Let me get me vest off!

SNIPERS: (*Sing and dance.*)
    But she's one hundred miles away
    One hundred miles from this horrible town
    And I feel like I want to take my rifle in my arms
    And shoot some bastard down

SNIPER ONE: What'll you do after the war?

SNIPER TWO: Been away from home three years. Used to live on a farm. I was right soft. Couldn't cut a chicken's throat. Now I could kill anything. But I don't know I could go back. I wouldn't know how to talk to normal people.

SNIPER ONE: We're bloody normal.

SNIPER TWO: We're killers.

SNIPER ONE: We're bloody normal killers.

SNIPER THREE: I saw them burn down my house. They killed everyone who tried to get out. I got my turn. I torched one of their houses. Yeah. Slept really well that night.

SERGEANT: You know what I'd like to see? I'd like to see that town torn up into little pieces. I want to bash into that town with mortars and bombs and machine guns. One day I'll ride through the streets in a tank and they'll all be screaming.

SNIPER ONE: And you'll be laughing, right?

SERGEANT: Right.

SNIPER FOUR: I don't hate em. But I'm proud to fight for my country. Days when nothing much happens I get a bit scared cos I worry about dying. Then I wish I was one of those kids that stay in bomb shelters all day.

SERGEANT: You're safer up here with a gun. How old are you, kid?

SNIPER FOUR: Thirteen, Serge.

SNIPER ONE: (*Holding up a hand.*) Listen.

Fade out lights on the hill and the snipers.

SCENE SIX

PARTY TIME TWO

Swados house.

Preparations for the party almost complete. JAMES working on big painted sculpture. LUCY moulding a plaster statue beside him. MELANIE and ELLI sewing costumes – by hand. GABY building a tree. KARL writing in notebook.

LUCY: (*Looking at JAMES' sculpture.*) It's wild, James. What's it going to be?

JAMES: Newfoundland dog on a mountain bike.

LUCY: That's great.

KARL: What's a Newfoundland dog doing on a bloody mountain bike?

LUCY: Riding it, bumface.

KARL: Just asking.

LUCY: What you going to do, James? I mean after the siege.

JAMES: I'll cycle from San Francisco to New York and start a rock band. You can come with me, Lucy.

LUCY: What sort of bike'll I need?

Enter SALLY, with plastic shopping bag, slowly. She wears a white dove.

ELLI: Mum. How's Ingrid?

SALLY: They shot her. Broke her arm.

ELLI: Who did?

SALLY: Jameson's thugs. They wouldn't let me talk to her. Said she's under arrest. They had her chained to a hospital bed. They're going to put her on trial.

GABY: What for? Ingrid's been working herself to bits round the clock picking shrapnel out of people's backs and strapping broken bones together and saving kids lives, she's one of the few people in this town who's any bloody use, what're they doing her for?

SALLY: I dunno. Undermining morale, giving comfort to the enemy, I dunno. (*Sits down.*) Anyway, I got oranges and apples on the way back. For the twins' birthday party.

MIKE Swados, aged 18, the eldest son of SALLY, comes in. He wears uniform and carries a kitbag. He is a bit drunk.

MIKE: Yeah! (*Hugs SALLY.*) Hey kids, it's your big brother, home just in time for the big party.

SALLY: You're all right?

GABY: You're not wounded? You're walking a bit funny.

MIKE: I've been drinking some funny wine. Hey, but
I've written a song for the party. A one and a two and
a three and a four –

THE STREETS OF HELL

(*Sings.*) The night is cold
The town is dead
I'm going out
Of my mixed-up head

The moon is down
The sky is black
I'm going out
And I won't be back

They say when you're old enough to rock-n-roll
You're old enough for any old thrill
You got the body and you got the soul
You old enough to kill

I gotta knife
I gotta gun
I'm going out
And have some fun

I gotta knife
I gotta gun
See my face
You better run

MIKE / BACKING GROUP: (*Sing.*)
They say when you're old enough to rock n roll
You're old enough for any old thrill
You got the body and you got the soul
You old enough to kill

MIKE: (*Sings.*) I got no home
I got no name

But I got guts
All full of flame

I'm going to walk
The streets of Hell
Until I fall
Like the others fell

MIKE / BACKING GROUP: (*Sing.*)
They say when you're old enough to rock n roll
You're old enough for any old thrill
You got the body and you got the soul
You old enough to kill.

They say when you're old enough to rock n roll
You're old enough for any old thrill
You got the body and you got the soul
You old enough to kill.

During this song Family and Friends join in with dancing and singing, despite the bleak words they perform it with huge energy and by the end they're really carried away. Doorbell rings.

MIKE: I'll get it. Bjork said she might drop in for a snog.

MIKE returns immediately with armed POLICEWOMAN.

POLICEWOMAN: Mrs Swados?

SALLY: That's me.

POLICEWOMAN: You're the mother of Betsy and Arlo Swados?

SALLY: Course I am.

ELLI: This is all going to be their birthday party. Their sixteenth.

POLICEWOMAN: Yes. They're not here, are they?

SALLY: They're down the Stargate Club.

POLICEWOMAN: No. They were spotted tonight climbing over the border fence and stealing a boat.

SALLY: They crossed the river?

GABY: Betsy and Arlo crossed the river?

POLICEWOMAN: That's what it looks like.

MIKE: Happy birthday, sweet sixteen.

Family and friends in shock. They put down whatever they've been working on and stare at each other in disbelief.

SCENE SEVEN

CROSSING THE RIVER

On main stage and in hills

A wood, with actors playing the trees, occupies most of stage right. Beyond the wood, from the hills of the higher stage, the river – of blue cloth – runs to downstage left and out, through the audience if possible. On the river, hidden by 'trees' is a boat. Dawn is breaking. TWINS enter from upstage right again. On the hills above there are also lights on the four SNIPERS and their SERGEANT.

BETSY: Not far now.

ARLO: Polecat Wood.

BETSY: Soon be light.

ARLO: Maybe we should rest. Hide out for a bit.

BETSY: Better keep going.

ARLO: Could be miles.

BETSY: Look through the trees. See that shining? That's the river.

ARLO: I know what we have to do.

BETSY: What's that?

ARLO: Run from one tree to the next. Freeze. Then run again. Don't give the snipers a target. Like this. (*Runs and stops.*)

SNIPER ONE: Something down that wood, Serge.

SERGEANT looks through binoculars.

SERGEANT: Bloody bunny rabbits.

BETSY: (*Follows ARLO's example, stops by a tree near him.*) They'll see us moving. Go slower.

ARLO: (*On to next tree.*) We got cover.

SNIPER ONE: Somebody down there.

SNIPER TWO: Where?

SNIPER THREE: Got it! Hey. (*Fires twice.*)

BETSY: Slow down. They can track fast moves. Hit us when we get to the river. Slow down.

SNIPER FOUR: Bloody trees. Can't see for bloody trees.

SNIPER ONE: There's a gap.

Fires two shots. ARLO winces.

ARLO: OK, Betsy. Slowly does it.

They move from tree to tree slowly.

SERGEANT: Don't waste good ammo. Looks like two of 'em. Wait till they hit the riverbank. Then give 'em the wind in the willows.

BETSY: Sun's coming up.

SNIPER TWO: Sun's coming up.

ARLO: Have to sprint it.

The trees of the wood have been moving back, so that now there is an open space between the TWINS and the River, only a few trees hiding the boat.

BETSY: There's the willow trees. Wait. Wait. Wait. Run for it – now!

TWINS make a dash for the trees on the riverbank. SNIPERS fire, but TWINS manage to reach the cover of the trees. They pause.

Now we just hop in the boat and head downstream.

ARLO: I feel really shaky.

BETSY: Keep yourself together.

ARLO: No, I feel shaky but good. Half an hour's time we'll be safe. In a peace country.

BETSY: What'll we do there?

ARLO: Don't know yet. High Command'll tell me when we get there. Come on – the boat.

TWINS climb hurriedly into the boat. They begin to move it down stream with paddles or oars. But it doesn't move fast as it floats away from the hills and towards the other bank.

SERGEANT: Nice little boat. Two of 'em. Ready. Aim. Fire.

All SNIPERS fire. TWINS crouch down into the bottom of the boat. The bright white light of death – then blackout.

Clear the river, boat and Snipers' camp.

SCENE EIGHT

THE HALLS OF JUSTICE

A court and the street outside.

Outside the Town Courtroom, three or four young men and women are carrying home-made banners. They are standing still, a bit afraid, outside the court to protest. The lyrics they sing were mostly written by Roy Baker of Preston Manor High School, Wembley.

JUSTICE

PROTESTERS: (*Sing.*) Justice
All we ask
Is justice

Three men
Came to our house
At midnight
Three masked men
Came to our house
At midnight
They left our father dead

Justice
All we ask
Is justice

Three men
Knocked on our door
At midnight
Three men
Outside our house
By moonlight
They asked to see our father
They shot him in the head

Justice
All we ask
Is justice

Justice
All we ask
Is justice

People are moving into the court. Guards with small batons shove and bully the PROTESTERS out of the way. Among the people who move into the main area of the court are the SWADOS FAMILY – minus BETSY and ARLO of course – and their FRIENDS. They will stand or sit with the public CROWD in the court. Also on the main floor is the JURY – best if they bring their own seats. There will also be a Witness Stand and a Dock – probably just below the Higher Stage. On the Higher Stage will be a Chair for the Judge, lower Chair for Clerk of the Court. Prosecutor and Defence Lawyer to work from the main floor of the Court. GUARDS commanded by THUG TWO show the public CROWD to their places. FEATHERS, as Clerk of the Court, co-opted by the Jameson gang, stands on main floor. MIKE Swados, in uniform, is among the public. A few of the CROWD wear white doves.

FEATHERS: Order! Please. Yes – er – Silence in Court. Stand up for the Judge of the Civil Court of Arden.

CROWD still muttering.

THUG TWO: (*Shouts.*) Shut up, you lot! And stand up for the Judge.

FEATHERS: Thanks, Alphonse.

THUG TWO: Any time, Miss Feathers.

Enter Dr JAMESON as a Judge, in long wig and scarlet gown. Takes seat.

FEATHERS: The sheet of charges, Justice Jameson.

FEATHERS hands JAMESON a sheet of paper. JAMESON glances through it, then raps with gavel.

JAMESON: I call this court to order. The former court of Justice has been democratically dissolved. The people of this historic town have demanded an emergency court which can act swiftly and decisively to wipe out crime in Arden. (*Raps gavel.*) I call on the town Prosecutor.

The Town Prosecutor makes his entrance. He is the Rev MOUTH, in wig and gown. A gasp or two from the CROWD who hadn't expected such a loaded court.

MOUTH: Ladies and Gentlemen of the Jury, we don't want to waste your time or the time of those who guide and guard our beloved town. So I have agreed with the Defence Counsel, Mrs Channer, to keep all cases brief.

MRS CHANNER: (*Mild and slightly bewildered shopkeeper.*) Yes, that is correct. Brief.

JAMESON: Come on, then. First case.

FEATHERS: Call Edward Sandow.

THUG TWO: EDWARD SANDOW!

GUARDS bring in SANDOW, a small, lively young man.

JAMESON: Edward Sandow, you are charged with looting from a bombed house various items of food, how do you plead?

SANDOW: (*A fast talker.*) That wasn't looting. It was desperate. My sister's in the pudding club. She was crying and yelling: 'Get me some fruit.' So I nip round the market. Not a satsuma. She's screaming: 'Gimme fruit or I'm dead!' I try the Ration Board for pregnancy fruit. They chuck me out. On the way home there's this house with its front wall gone missing so I wander in and there's this cupboard in the wall and I kind of wedge it open. And it's choc-a-bloc full of tins of tangerines and pears and pineapple chunks.

MOUTH: So what did you do?

SANDOW: (*Demonstrating.*) Well I dropped down on my knees and shouted: Check this out! Hey, I've hit the jackpot. (*Kneeling, kisses his hands to God above.*) Thank you God, I deserve it. Yeah. And then this woman comes up behind me and she says:

HOUSEWOMAN: (*Giving evidence.*) What are you doing in my house? And he said:

SANDOW: Just checking that everything's OK, madam. Health inspection. Have to take a sample of these tins for tests at the lab.

HOUSEWOMAN: And then he just took half a dozen tins of mixed fruit and off he hops.

MRS CHANNER: Can you identify him?

HOUSEWOMAN: Course I can, that's Eddie Sandow, lives two streets away.

JAMESON: Right. No problems there. Jury, you have to take that as a Guilty plea. In which case you, the Foreman, should now tell me your verdict.

FOREMAN: (*Standing.*) Guilty, my Lord.

JAMESON: The accused Edward Sandow has been found guilty of looting during the emergency. Take him out, get him into uniform, send him to the front line.

SANDOW: I'm only fourteen! It's murder!

SANDOW, protesting is taken out.

JAMESON: And you, yes you, the woman with a cupboard full of fruit. That's what we call hoarding rationed food during an emergency and it carries an automatic fine of four hundred.

HOUSEWOMAN: But your honour –

JAMESON: Two weeks to pay. Next case.

FEATHERS: Call Jessie Nola.

THUG TWO: JESSIE NOLA!

JESSIE is brought into the dock. She's a young woman with a black eye, who has obviously been roughed up.

JESSIE: Guilty, your honour.

JAMESON: You haven't been charged yet.

FEATHERS: Jessie Nola, you are charged with selling illegal drugs. I believe you wish to enter a plea of Guilty.

JESSIE: That's right, Feathers, I mean your honour.

MRS CHANNER: In your defence, Jessie, what led you into the world of drugs?

JESSIE: (*Like a speech she has learned.*) Shortly after the siege began I became very stressed out. A friend suggested that I should smoke marijuana.

MRS CHANNER: And you did?

JESSIE: Yeah well everybody did. (*Reverting to her speech.*) In order to pay for the drugs I bought, I turned to selling substances myself.

MOUTH: When did you start dealing?

JESSIE: I was fifteen. Now I'm seventeen.

MOUTH: Do you feel guilty about selling to young children?

JESSIE: No, that's what they want.

MOUTH: How about the police?

JESSIE: Yeah I sell to them as well.

MOUTH: I understand that when you were arrested you had a gun?

JESSIE: Everybody got a gun. There's a siege on.

MOUTH: Would you use that gun to shoot anyone?

JESSIE: Yeah. If they tried to rip me off.

MOUTH: My lord, this defendant has admitted her guilt. And there are certain mitigating circumstances.

JESSIE smiles at him, there has evidently been a deal.

FOREMAN: We have to find her guilty, then?

FEATHERS: You're the jury – you can decide –

JAMESON: I am recording that as a Guilty verdict. But taking your age and circumstances into consideration, I sentence you to fourteen days working for care in the community.

JESSIE: Thank you, my lordship.

JESSIE joins public in the court.

JAMESON: Next case.

FEATHERS: Call Private Falla and Private Nandez.

THUG TWO: PRIVATE FALLA AND PRIVATE NANDEZ!

SNIPER THREE, who was bitter because he saw his house burn down, and SNIPER FOUR, who is only 13, are led into the dock. The CROWD recognise them as enemy soldiers and general hissing and quiet revulsion is in evidence from many, though not all. The two SNIPERS are both handcuffed and guarded. SNIPER THREE holds his head up and stares straight ahead. SNIPER FOUR glances around nervously, bows his head. One side of his face is badly bruised.

MOUTH: You two – Falla and Nandez. You are charged with the deliberate murder of citizens of Arden.

SNIPER THREE: We don't murder. We are soldiers with the Army of Free Dower.

Hisses.

MOUTH: Private Falla, you were captured after a fire fight in the hills. You had a little hide-out up there, didn't you? A sniper's perch?

CROWD: (*Mutters of Snipers etc.*)

SNIPER THREE: Any soldier's a sniper when he's ordered to be a sniper.

MOUTH: You're just little toy snipers – wind you up and you shoot women and children.

SNIPER THREE: Soldiers shoot the enemy. Your lot shot at us. That's OK. We all got a job to do. I shoot people. I get shot at.

JAMESON: What about the other one? Nandez?

SNIPER FOUR: Sir.

MOUTH: How old are you, Nandez?

SNIPER FOUR: Thirteen, sir. Been a soldier since I was eleven.

MOUTH: And how many people have you killed, Nandez?

SNIPER FOUR: I think I've killed six so far.

MRS CHANNER: How did you get in the army at eleven years old?

SNIPER FOUR: My mum and dad got killed early on. So I was just wandering around nicking stuff to eat.

Then the army gave me regular hot meals and a place to sleep. The army's like a family to me. Yes. It's my home, the army is.

MRS CHANNER: What's that on the side of your face?

SNIPER FOUR: I got it from falling down.

MRS CHANNER: Nobody pushed you?

SNIPER FOUR: No, I just fell down on the side of my face.

SNIPER THREE: We didn't break any law. There's a war on. There's Geneva conventions. We've got rights —

FEATHERS: Excuse me your honour. I'm getting a bit lost. Are we doing a war crimes trial now?

JAMESON: (*Gently.*) Please don't worry about technicalities. (*Exploding.*) I'm trying to run a town under siege, not a bleeding nursery school.

FOREMAN: Some of the jury are rather worried, your honour —

MOUTH: If they're that worried they can dismiss themselves! My lord, I am content for the verdict to be postponed —

JAMESON: Great. That's fine. Put 'em in the Horrordrome. Army of Free Dower! Keep 'em in chains. (*To SNIPERS.*) I'll visit you later for a chat about the Geneva Conventions. Next case!

CROWD is a bit disconcerted and divided by the Snipers' trial. Justice is being seen to be pretty haphazard in this court. INGRID, one arm in a sling, is brought into the dock.

MOUTH: Good morning, Dr Simmons.

She stares at him, says nothing.

FEATHERS: Doctor Ingrid Simmons, you are accused of spreading alarm and despondency among the citizens of Arden by making defeatist speeches in public during an extreme emergency, and also attempting to assault the Governor of the city, how do you plead?

INGRID is silent.

Guilty or not guilty?

No reply.

JAMESON: She doesn't know. Carry on. First witness.

THUG ONE: (*Steps on to the witness stand.*) On the day in question I was on duty in the market square providing protection for the Governor of Arden when I observed the accused addressing members of the public.

MOUTH: And did you make a note of what she said?

THUG ONE: I did sir. (*Produces notebook.*) She said that she had decided not to kill anyone whatever the cause. She invited others to do the same.

MOUTH: A clear breach of the Emergency Orders Act, I believe?

JAMESON: Outrageous.

MOUTH: What happened next?

THUG ONE: The Governor attempted to reason with the accused.

MOUTH: And what did she do?

THUG ONE: She tried to attack the Governor. So I shot her in the arm.

MRS CHANNER: Did she open fire first?

THUG ONE: I didn't let her. I retaliated before she could get a gun. You got to be quick these days.

MRS CHANNER: She wasn't armed, was she?

THUG ONE: I wasn't to know that, I'm not psychic. She was coming at the Governor.

MRS CHANNER: Walking towards the Governor.

THUG ONE: Walking in a threatening manner.

MRS CHANNER: So you shot her?

THUG ONE: Yeah.

MRS CHANNER: Three times?

THUG ONE: Well yeah.

JAMESON: All right. Dr Simmons, we've got precious little time. But before I sentence you –

FOREMAN: Pardon me, your honour, but we haven't reached a verdict.

MOUTH: This is a case involving national security. Not a jury matter. The judge pronounces both verdict and sentence.

FOREMAN: On behalf of the jury, I protest.

FEATHERS: I think you're right.

INGRID: We could live together in peace in this town. We could live in peace with the people who besiege us now. All religions, all races, all nationalities – we're all human beings. There's been some talk about courage today, well I admire courage, the courage of those on both sides who are brave enough to refuse to kill. Blessed are the peacemakers. But the peace movement is being crushed by bullies like you, Jameson, little gangsters with big egos who divide people from people and scare them into killing each other so you can seize power. You are the cause of this war. You are the siege. Have you no shame at all?

An outcry from JAMESON and his friends. But this is drowned by most of the people in the court. THUG ONE moves towards INGRID. His way is blocked by MIKE and FEATHERS.

FEATHERS: (*Now wearing a white dove.*) Lay off her, thug.

MIKE: (*Also wearing white dove.*) Sit down and listen. (*He pushes THUG ONE into a seat.*)

TAKES A LONG TIME

INGRID: (*Sings.*) Once upon a time
There was a mighty forest
From Southampton to the Hebrides.
But the human race
Brought axes and saws
And began their war against the trees
Year after year
Century by century
They cut down every tree in their way
Branch after branch
And tree after tree
Till the forest was transformed
Into concrete cities
Where the streets and the faces are grey.

INGRID / CHORUS: (*Sing.*) Took a long time
Took a long long time
But they cut them all down in the end
Took a long time
Took a long long time
But they cut them all down in the end

INGRID: (*Sings.*) Once upon a time
I knew a man and a woman
Planted seven hundred trees a year
Now their seven kids

Are planters as well
See the mighty forest reappear

INGRID / A FEW OTHERS: (*Sing.*) Year after year
Century by century
Our woodlands will be slowly re-made
Branch after branch
And tree after tree
Till this country is transformed
To a flowering forest
And the creatures will sing in its shade.

INGRID / CHORUS: (*Sing.*) Takes a long time
Takes a long long time
But the trees will return in the end
Takes a long time
Takes a long long time
But peace will prevail in the end
Takes a long time
Takes a long long time –

INGRID: And a hell of a lot of patient and courageous
work –

INGRID / CHORUS: (*Sing.*)
But peace will prevail in the end,
Yes peace will prevail in the end.

MOUTH: (*Yells.*) Silence in Court! Silence!

*And there is silence for a second. BETSY enters, in some sort
of shock, blood on her clothes. She goes to INGRID and takes
her hand. SALLY and GABY rush up to BETSY.*

SALLY: Are you all right?

BETSY nods.

Where's Arlo?

GABY: What happened? They said you crossed the river.

BETSY: We crossed the border. Started to cross the river.

SALLY: Where's Arlo?

MOUTH: You're a deserter!

JAMESON: A traitor. Don't you know there's a war on?

BETSY: Oh yes. My father's dead because of your war. And now my brother's dead because of your war. But I don't want revenge. There are enough dead fathers and brothers on the other side to pay for my Dad and Arlo.

SALLY: Arlo.

BETSY: We nearly made it. They shot him down.

The SWADOS family move into a circle, arms around each other – a slow movement in total silence. Finally INGRID speaks.

INGRID: What can we do?

White doves are appearing on people all around.

BETSY: It's Arlo's sixteenth birthday. I would like you all to come and help me bury him.

GABY: We've made a sort of jungle for you and Arlo. For your birthday.

SALLY: We'll bury Arlo in the jungle. It's very beautiful.

BETSY: Yes, he'd like that.

JAMESON: I call this court to order.

MOUTH: ORDER!

BETSY: Come on. Let's go and see this jungle. (*Takes out a piece of paper.*) Arlo left a poem explaining how he wanted to be buried.

Almost ALL the crowd, including CLERK and MRS CHANNER, follow BETSY, INGRID and GABY from the courtroom, turning their backs on JAMESON, MOUTH and the TWO THUGS.

JAMESON: Come back! You'll pay for this!

SCENE NINE

THE JUNGLE OF ARDEN

Music. All the cast gradually assemble, filling both the stages with the Jungle. There will be giant flowers, trees, animals, birds, fish and reptiles of all kinds, a waterfall – whatever it takes to make a very crowded, varied, wonderful jungle of things. These may be two dimensional pieces of wood painted, or three-dimensional sculptures constructed out of all kinds of junk – but the more the better. There should be no attempt to impose an overall style. Each contribution is a personal contribution to the twins' birthday. It would be great if primary school children could become involved in this part of the project and make their own creatures and plants for the Jungle. While the Jungle is being assembled the orchard of blossoms from the first scene is reconstructed on the higher stage.

It is night and a moon and stars appear.

About half-way through the assembling of the Jungle, friends bring ARLO in in a cardboard coffin shaped like a rowing boat. BETSY stands beside the coffin as it is put down.

BETSY: My brother Arlo wrote this poem. It tells us exactly how he wanted to be buried.

CARDBOARD ROWING BOAT

BETSY: (*Sings.*) All I know
Is that when I go
I will stand beside an unknown sea

And that's why I ask my best friends
When I die won't you make for me –

ARLO steps out of the coffin and stands with her.

BETSY / ARLO: (*Sing.*) A cardboard rowing boat
    For my coffin
    Painted in greens and blues
    And dress me up in my
    Faded denim
    And my favourite running shoes
    In my green and blue
    Cardboard rowing boat

    The poems of Blake in my
    Left hand pocket
    Navy rum in my right
    And in my hand put an eating apple
    And bury me late at night
    In my green and blue
    Cardboard rowing boat

    And I'll row away
    Cross that starry sea
    Singing and drifting with the tide
    And I'll row away
    And maybe I'll meet you at the other side
    In my green and blue
    Cardboard rowing boat

ALL: (*Sing.*) And I'll row away
    Cross that starry sea
    Singing and drifting with the tide
    And I'll row away
    And maybe I'll meet you at the other side
    In my green and blue
    Cardboard rowing boat...

The building of the Jungle continues. ARLO and BETSY join their family up in the orchard on the higher stage – as in the very first scene of the play. INGRID and GABY are still building Jungle.

GABY: When the siege is over, what's the first thing you'll do?

INGRID: I'm going to drink a whole pot of strong black real coffee.

GABY: I'm going to eat a whole box of chocolates.

INGRID: I'm going to buy a hardback book.

GABY: I'm going to the seaside and paddle and mess about.

INGRID: I'm going to go for a long drive – an hour or two hours or three hours.

GABY: I'm going to walk up into the hills and eat with my friends in their orchard.

INGRID: Come on then, let's go.

INGRID and GABY join the SWADOS family in the orchard.

THE JUNGLE OF ARDEN

COMPANY: (*Sing as they continue to build the Jungle of Arden. Lines may be divided among individuals in verses.*)

High above the jungle of Arden
The hill is misty and steep
In the yellow sun of the morning
It looks like a lion asleep

All the hillside pathways are zig-zag
It's easy losing your way
But we will climb up to our orchard
To witness the blossoms of May

Sitting round a table under pink and white trees
Eating very slowly, enjoying each bite
Sitting round a table with our memories
Terrible and happy, from morning till night

Sitting round a table under pink and white trees
On a hill above the jungle of Arden
Sitting round and arguing the rights and the wrongs.
Pass the roly-poly. Let's have some more cheese.

Harmonising sweetly on our favourite songs.
Drinking wine together, the pink and the white –
Sitting round a table under pink and white trees
On a hill above the jungle of Arden.

*Another peaceful day
Feels like another peaceful day
And the nightmare's flown away
And it's another peaceful day
On a hill above the jungle of Arden.

*The stages have now become a bright and overflowing jungle
– an image of radiant, chaotic and creative peace. Let's dance.*

The End.

* This chorus sung in counterpoint with the two Sitting Round verses

About *the siege*

HOW THE SIEGE BEGAN

Way back in 1994, Tamsyn Imison, the head teacher of Hampstead School and her drama teacher, Jenny Johnson, were lamenting the lack of good plays for teenagers to perform. They decided to see if they could commission a new one. The playwright David Edgar advised them they'd have to pay properly to make it possible for a good writer to spend the time it would take to create an epic. It was decided to get together with 19 other schools, all over England. Each school would contribute, initially, £500, and each school would mount its own production in 1996 or 1997. The play would then be published and would be available for other groups to perform. David suggested me as the playwright.

I jumped at the chance, partly because the idea of writing for companies of up to 200 was very exciting in our cut-back era of one-person plays, partly because I had an idea at the back of my head. I wanted to write a totally modern version of Cervantes' great and neglected tragedy *The Siege of Numantia*. I was encouraged by the recent achievements of the playwrights Trevor Griffiths in *The Gulf Between Us* (about the Gulf War) and Caryl Churchill's *Mad Forest* (about Romania.)

All along, Tamsyn has been determined, against all the sensible odds, to make this epic work and she has given it every kind of energy and encouragement. All of us in the scheme owe her a tremendous debt. She is as unstoppable as an earthquake – a very benevolent earthquake.

Tamsyn and Jenny and I talked. They moved into action and soon we had our first meeting with teachers from other interested schools.

DECISION TIME

Meeting at Impington Village College, Cambridge, November 12th 1994 with a group of interested teachers. I went along with a strong idea for a theme and story in my head, but I was ready to jettison it if something more exciting came up. Before I revealed my idea, I asked the teachers what sort of subjects most interested or affected their pupils. Their answers included:

The many sides of a story in the media
Social problems
Homelessness
Grief
Aids
Gangland in the 1920s
Murder
Mystery
Comedy
Horror
Drugs and police
Bear killing
Prejudice
Emergent Eastern Europe
Children's rights in Brazil
Drugs
Impossibility of finding work
War and violence
The need to belong to a nation, a family, a team, a club and the fragmentation of community.

HUMOUR

At this point I suggested the theme of people in a modern city under siege. We talked about the blockade of Cuba, the sanctions on Iraq, the current sieges in Sarajevo and Africa.

I said I was determined that, whatever horrors the play might depict, it should end affirmatively. I was concerned to express the heroic work of local peace movements, which have always been active though often under-publicised, in modern wars from Asia to Europe. Though we would show a family and a community in wartime, we would conclude by celebrating the possibilities of peace.

I said we'd try to show what happens to morality and belief in a siege.

Somebody said: Many students feel there's no escape from the estate where they live. The age you are is less important than your ability to manage. All must become guardians. Young children have the enormous burden of looking after those younger and sometimes the very old.

Somebody said: Attitudes to stealing change if your mother is ill and can't pay. But do you steal from next door or from the rich?

I said I believed that many of the themes we'd mentioned or discussed would emerge in the story of a siege. The teachers agreed and were very positive about this idea.

We needed songs – to move the play along, to express high emotion whether happy or sad, to unite the cast. I proposed Andrew Dickson. Andrew has written the music for several Mike Leigh movies, performed many times with the People Show and collaborated with Anne Jellicoe on giant community shows. I've worked with him as composer on several TV plays and stage shows and I knew him as the least egocentric of composers, who can magic singing and instrumental work out of the least likely subjects.

It was decided to hold two waves of five or six workshops, each to be attended by teachers and pupils from three or four schools. The first wave would be dedicated to the writing and improvisation of material for the script.

The second wave, which the composer would also attend, would be concerned with performance and wouldn't be held until the script was in its first draft.

THE WRITING

At home I equipped myself with a stack of London Library books covering sieges of all ages – Jerusalem, Masada, Paris, Leningrad. I followed contemporary sieges, particularly Sarajevo.

From the first wave workshops I took poems, scenes and speeches written by students. A few are incorporated whole in the script and their authors are credited, but often they didn't quite fit stylistically.

During improvisations I took lavish notes and several situations and characters came out of these, especially in the market and courtroom scenes. I also hung around at lunchtime, taking notes on the jokes, ideas, teasing and slang of the students – I don't have any teenagers of my own at the moment.

A great deal of this material I typed up on my Apple Mac and printed it out. I then hacked it into pieces and threw out the words I knew I didn't need any more.

I re-made the shape of the original simple story by using the Card Method. This meant taking a stack of library cards and filling each with the name of a scene, the characters, any songs and other vital information. Then I arranged the scenes in a tentative order all over the floor after shutting my golden retriever out. I examined the scenes, shuffled them, tried different juxtapositions and threw out the least necessary scenes, trying to keep the story of the Swados family and the story of the town itself both running.

Then I wrote the play, scene by scene, each scene backed by a folder of documentary and imaginative material.

I was just starting to write the first scene when, in November 1995, we had a terrible family tragedy. I had to stop any work for two months and at one time felt I couldn't write the play. But too many people had already given too much, and they couldn't be abandoned. So the play was written and then, as the result of the Second Wave of workshops, somewhat rewritten.

In most of the Second Wave workshops the script was ready and we read aloud either the first act or the entire script of the play.

But most of the work was done by Andrew Dickson, our composer. He would appear in his amazing green and blue jeans with his box of musical tricks. He'd give an intensive and enjoyable warm up.

Andrew spoke of ways of creating sound effects and sound collages without tape. Using found objects. There is a thing where you shake a box of Smarties, eat a Smartie and shake again, and the noise changes.

He showed us how to create a dawn chorus in orchard, hospital, supermarket and war noises.

He produced instruments which whizz round on strings, and look extremely dangerous, while sounding angelic. Also the very popular Yalophone made out of tuned front-door keys.

'If you begin together and finish together it doesn't matter what you do in the middle,' said Andrew to one group. Andrew approaches any group as a crowd of very talented friends.

One of the most important achievements of the Second Wave workshops was to establish three or four songs firmly in the school's repertoire, not just knowing the songs but understanding their purpose.

Response to the songs was very strong and positive, not just to the rocky fun numbers like 'You Got Twins', but also to the elegiac 'Cardboard Rowing Boat', which I believe is one of the most cheerful songs about death ever written.

ANDREW DICKSON ON THE SIEGE

I love writing tunes for Adrian's words. It's a challenge, the only hazard being that they tend to just plop into place with minimum effort. This is because the lyrics are so expertly crafted with their own natural rhythms that they almost sing themselves. As a result, I hope that the tunes for *the siege* are neither too plain nor yet too complicated. My intention is that they should be sung straight, with whatever backing is available – solo guitar, rock group, chamber orchestra or dijeridoo. Harmonies and extra parts are an added luxury. The mood of the music must reflect the contents of the songs and help to drive the show along. Adrian's songs are strongly narrative, and an integral part of the action, so must never let the story sag or the audience shuffle.

the siege is a powerful story of real people and real feelings, therefore the music and noises should be as real as possible too. Try to create sound effects organically, using voices, acoustic instruments and props, and when rhythms are called for, play the set, as well as any percussion instruments you can get. I work on the assumption that if you have a heart beat – a sense of rhythm – then you are musical. So everyone can be involved in the creation of music and atmosphere for this show. It has been an exciting and moving experience to work on *the siege.* Thanks Adrian and Tamsyn, and Good Luck Musicians. Go for it. Break out.

TAMSYN IMISON ON THE SIEGE – A CO-OPERATIVE VENTURE

On the programme for Sinfin Community School Derby's last production in July '96 it says *the siege* a play inspired by the National Playwright Commissioning Group. The vigour and enthusiasm of the students and the obvious enjoyment of the staff involved in this co-operative venture between twenty schools, a playwright and a composer are making this ambitious venture well worthwhile.

The Commissioning Group is a first and was initiated by teachers at Hampstead School London, as the impoverished school's answer to accessing writers and composers and getting plays and music to perform that are appropriate, immediate and fun. Few schools can afford to raise the thirty thousand pounds that the group of twenty schools across the country have raised between them in order to commission their own play from the leading playwright Adrian Mitchell and the composer Andrew Dickson.

The play was written after the writer and composer had worked with students from each of the schools. The workshops were exciting opportunities for learning how a play is conceived and written. The school's contributions are recognised in the text. The music involves all those taking part and is a welcome change from the usual repertoire. It has also inspired good work in English, history, geography and the creative arts. The whole process has been challenging but unexpected bonuses have also come from mixing talented creative arts co-ordinators and the varied groups of young people at the workshops and planning meetings as well as unique opportunities to see and learn from each other's productions.

The play has already attracted lots of artistic and media interest. In the current competitive climate it is brilliant to see how well a co-operative venture like this pays off. Everyone wins, but most of all, our young people get to experience the creative process and value the Arts.

Tamsyn Imison is the Head Teacher of Hampstead School, co-ordinators of the *siege* project.

SCHOOLS NATIONAL PLAYWRIGHT COMMISSIONING GROUP FOUNDER MEMBERS

Attleborough High School, Norwich.
Camfield High School, Wigan.
Durham Johnston Comprehensive, Durham.
Hampstead School, London.
Henry Court School, Hampshire.
Hinchingbrooke School, Huntingdon.
Ilkeston School, Derby.
Impington Village College, Cambridge.
Outwood Grange School, Wakefield.
Peers School, Oxford.
Preston Manor School, Wembley.

Sconce Hills High School, Nottinghamshire.
Sinfin Community School, Derby.
Stroud High School, Gloucestershire.
Winchmore School, Hertfordshire.

ASSOCIATE SCHOOLS

King Edward VI School, Northumberland.
Beauchamp College, Leicester.
Townsend School, St Albans.
Cranford Community School.
Banwell School, Stevenage.
Blatchington Mill School, Sussex.

Production Notes

CASTING AND SONGS

Any part in this play can be played by an actor of any racial origin. This includes members of the central Swados family. (Pronounce it Swaydoss.)

Many parts in the play can be played as either male or female. This is deliberate. The political gangster, Dr Jameson, for instance, can be a man or a woman.

Sometimes a song may be sung by somebody other than the designated actor. Sometimes – as in the case of Ingrid – it's very important that the character should be a particularly strong singer. But you could cast two Ingrids, one to act and one to sing, wearing identical costumes and taking over from each other in clear view of the audience.

Songs are an integral part of the show and no named part should be cast without making sure whether they will be called upon to sing solo or not. It's not a musical as such, but a play with songs. So please test all singing voices before casting.

Most of the songs are there for a defined dramatic purpose. They occur at the moment when emotions become too high for speech to be adequate, a kind of overflowing into emotion. They are intended to carry the story forward, not to stop the show as in conventional music. There are some songs which may well become 'production numbers' – with extended dance routines, special costumes, effects etc. 'You Got Twins' is one example, the 'Boy Band' routine of the Snipers is another.

Songs should be worked on at every rehearsal, even if there's only time to go through the mass choruses once.

Whatever the musical backing, the words of all the songs must be heard all the time. If there's any electronic music around, this will mean there must be microphones – which will probably be necessary in any case. Radio mikes are favourite.

MINIMAL PROPS

Heavy pieces of wood painted black can be much more interesting weapons than accurately reproduced models of automatic rifles, big guns etc. Anyway I don't want to encourage anyone to spend time making perfect reproductions of weapons of death.

We do need a sofa and an armchair for the TV watching family. The sofa and the armchair are reversible and should have sandbags on the other side so they can convert instantly into a gun emplacement/sniper nest. But usually let's have minimum furniture and simple props. It may be good to have blossoms of orchard trees on some kind of camouflage netting. Maybe this can be replaced by wartime netting or maybe simply reversed.

ARRANGING HALL AREA AND THE JUNGLE OF ARDEN

If using a school hall, suggest using as main acting area a large square piece of floor right in front of the stage. The audience sits on three sides of this area, which represents the besieged town itself. Upper stage to be used as a hillside above the town for: Orchard in the hills, gun and sniper emplacement and besieging army. Also for reactions in a safe country far from the siege – a sitting room with family watching TV etc. Blossoms for first and last scene. Otherwise broken trees and gun barrels, sandbags.

Final Jungle of Arden scene to overflow, using both stage and floor areas. A great garden to be made, with flowers, beasts, birds etc all as big as people and painted in bright colours. Everybody connected with the production should make at least one piece for this Jungle – it should be amazing.

The first brief should be – make a tree, a flower, a creature or a person as big or bigger than yourself. This is a good challenge and will help avoid skimpy little models.

The pieces for the jungle can be made out of any old junk, which can then be painted with cheap poster paints. It should look bright and chaotic, a total mixture of styles and images. Peter Blake's cover for the Sergeant Pepper album is one model.

Also find inspiration in the work of untrained artists all over the world who have built Gardens of Eden in their back gardens, or amazing 'follies'. The art magazine *Raw Vision* is a great source of images, so are any books on 'primitive' and untrained artists.

For practical guidance in such arts as creating lanterns in the shape of birds and animals – consult *Engineers of the Imagination* (Methuen), a handbook based on the work of Welfare State International which gives clear diagrams and instructions.

Good to recruit pupils from a local primary school to make pieces for the Jungle.

OTHER DESIGN

It's intended that the first scene of the play, the orchard, should be very bright to look at, an orchard in blossom in the sunshine, with, if possible, blue sky beyond.

But for the main part of the show design should be austere, with a limited range of colours, to reflect the severity of the siege. (This can be broken by such numbers as 'You Got Twins', when we jump out of realistic mode into a production number.)

If the colours are generally restrained, this means that the overflowing colours of the final Jungle of Arden scene will make a strong emotional statement. (The blossoms should also return in that final scene.)

CROWD SCENES

There are several scenes – notably the market, the courtroom scene, the queueing scene and the Jungle of Arden – in which a lot of people take part, and often the crowd is a crucial character, whose mood changes a scene – as in the court. So a good deal of time should be spent working with the crowd, who also sing in the big choruses, explaining how they can help, sometimes with sound effects, or movements.

INFORMACTING

Suppose you are going to play a five-year-old child called Jan. It's better to say my name is Jan and I am five and concentrate on that child's character and words and actions than to do realistic costume and make-up and lisping, little child acting. Act the awareness of a little child. Concentrate on the truth of what is being said.

You may have to give a speech about terrible things which have happened to your character or which your character had seen. The worst thing you can do is sob your way through, or become all emotionally breathless. Remember you are a witness and you want to communicate facts. Think of reporters speaking straight to camera after witnessing horror, or people speaking straight to camera who have lost a loved one when they speak flatly, in shock, and the facts become clearer and clearer. If the actor emotes and sobs, the actor is saying look at me, how much I suffer. I don't want to know how much the actor is suffering. As an audience, I want to know the facts, as clearly as possible. Then let me decide, as an audience, whether I weep or not. Don't do my weeping for me, or tell me when to weep. Scenes of grief should be formalised.

KEEP TO THE SCRIPT

The playwright is open, up till your first night, to consider changes in the script. But please consult him – his name is on the script so he has to take the rap.

Please ask him about any cuts or changes you want to make to the script. (Best to save these till you have a collection to send him.)

Please discourage ad libs and added gags. It is better if crowds in scenes like the queueing or the courtroom show their reactions with sounds rather than words.

WHAT HAPPENS

Bidisha of Preston Manor, Wembley, wrote:

We watch through the hole in our wall at what seems to be a picture of war but step outside and you know that this is no picture. It is reality. Sieges, things that you hear about and think it can't happen to you. What happens when it does happen to you?

DEATH IN THE PLAY

Represented by a bright light and a freeze of all cast for three seconds. Save very bright light for this.

ENTRY TO PLAY AREA

Tickets may be exchanged outside by bureaucrats, icy, in suits, spectacles. Security.

On entry to hall, papers checked by soldiers.

MUSIC

Musicians to be visible, preferably on floor, backs to stage. Microphones to be used by solo singers. Balance to favour singers over instruments. Sounds of nature and warfare to be made by actors rather than tapes.

SOURCES OF THE PLAY

TV, radio, newspapers and magazine reports of current wars and sieges in Europe and Africa have been important. I've read many books about contemporary and historical sieges and it was often horrifying reading – with occasional unexpected acts of mercy and compassion shining through. Diaries kept during the siege of Leningrad and accounts of the siege of Sarajevo by friends and strangers were essential to the project.

In workshops with all the schools, pupils and staff created improvisations, poems, stories and scenes based on the outline of the story. These have been invaluable. Occasionally I have used one of these contributions directly in the script, and when I have, the source is noted. But it would be impossible to note all the characters, incidents, speeches and jokes which I noted down in the first round of workshops and which I used. There were many pieces written which I admired greatly but couldn't include because, for reasons of story-flow or style, they didn't fit. The spirit and dedication of the people I've worked with in schools has been a great source of inspiration. Thank you.

Several of the characters are based on ideas by Claire Ferguson, Claire Gater and Gemma Brothers from Durham. Some others have arisen from many different improvisations by many different schools.

More helpful to me than anyone else have been two friends whom I met in Singapore. They are Marija and Kevin Sullivan. During the siege she was working on the newspaper *Oslobodjenje* in her home town, Sarajevo and also in the local peace movement. There she met Kevin Sullivan, a Scottish reporter covering the war until his leg was broken by a land-mine. They married and moved to Singapore.

They mustn't be blamed for any shortcomings of the play. But they have corresponded with me patiently, explaining things to me, supplying me with stories and ideas and understanding.

My warmest thanks to them.

Background to the Scenes

AN ORCHARD IN THE HILLS

This started when, about 15 years ago, I attended a poetry festival in Sarajevo. One of the things I liked best about that city, then at peace, was the way in which families sat in little orchards in the hills eating together. It seemed like a perfect image for peace.

TO LIBERATE ARDEN

A press conference based on many I've watched over the past few years, especially in the build-up to the Gulf War. Some of the quotes are taken directly from statements made by Generals.

MORNING UNDER SIEGE

Much of this account of day by day life under siege is based on diaries kept by people during the Second World War siege of Leningrad and also reports of the siege of Paris in the 1870s. I also remembered how, during World War Two, my mother, my brother and I, evacuated to a village near Bath, used to queue every Saturday morning for hours to buy bread, vegetables and meat.

AN IMAGINARY FEAST

Again this came from my childhood experience in the war, when our richest fantasies were often about bananas and oranges, bright fruit which we hadn't seen for years and could hardly remember.

TO THE DEATH

The take-over of power by politicians who appear respectable but turn out to be racist brutes is so common all over the world that there's no particular model for Jameson and Mouth. But every place of conflict – Northern Ireland or Sarajevo – there is always a peace movement. I determined to give those who work for peace the spotlight, for a change.

THE OPEN SCHOOL

The idea came, as so many have, from reports on school life in Sarajevo. IMPORTANT NOTE: ARDEN IS NOT SARAJEVO. I didn't, in the first place, feel qualified to write about the siege of Sarajevo. I didn't know it well enough, and that brave city has enough fine writers of its own. But I was very willing to learn from Sarajevo in my attempts to write about a British city, in a kind of alternative England, which is besieged by an army from a neighbouring province. (Say an alternative England in which the old deadly rivalries between Yorkshire and Lancashire returned.)

BIRTHDAY PLANS

One of the things which has impressed me most about the courage of people under siege is the way in which they refuse to be ground down into misery, but continually seek ways of celebrating whatever's left to celebrate. So a group of friends determined to hold a birthday party under impossible conditions seemed to me a good starting point for a play.

MOONCRATER MARKET

Much of the material comes from film documentaries, but even more comes from improvisations in the first group of workshops.

Material about drugs, here and elsewhere, comes partly from the terrible experience of some of the users close to me. The schizophrenia of one of them was apparently precipitated by drugs. The other died of an accidental overdose – see my new book of poems, *Blue Coffee*, for details.

LEAVING NOW

In most accounts of sieges I have read there have been stories of complicated escape routes involving tunnels, boats etc.

THE POWTEX ARMS FAIR, SNIPERS ON THE HILLS

Mostly based on press interviews with soldiers, but some of the quotes from pieces written in school workshops.

THE HALLS OF JUSTICE

Much of this based on improvisations in school workshops.

THE JUNGLE OF ARDEN

The idea of the cardboard rowing boat as a coffin really came from the efforts of the company Welfare State International to make funerals more human, cheap and artistically satisfying. One of their ideas is to have coffins made of cheap material painted to look beautiful by friends. See their excellent *The Dead Good Funerals Book* by Sue Gill and John Fox.

The whole scene should take its time to build, as the whole hall and stage is gradually filled with bright images of plants, flowers, trees, animals, birds, fish, insects and people.

It should show how human beings, even in extreme conditions, can still express their love for each other and their love for our planet through art, and state their opposition to killing and war through art.